xpand EXPERIENCING CHRISTIANITY

Richard Reichert

Ave Maria Press
Notre Dame, Indiana 46556

Nihil Obstat: John L. Reedy, C.S.C.
        Censor Deputatus

Imprimatur: Most Rev. Leo A. Pursley, D.D.
        Bishop of Fort Wayne-South Bend

Library of Congress Catalog Card Number: 72-137680
ISBN: 0-87793-027-9

Design: Chet Sygiel

Printed in the United States of America

ABOUT THIS BOOK

X-PAND: Experiencing Christianity is a group-centered religious education program for high school students (ninth through 11th grades). It was designed as a handbook for teachers (discussion leaders) who wish to work with small groups in informal settings in the home or classroom.

The text consists of a series of lessons on the pivotal elements in human and religious development of the Christian. The lessons have two special qualities. First, they are tailored to suit the informal, small group settings popular in catechetical programs today. Second, they employ various group dynamic exercises which *involve* the student in the topic under discussion. Because the lessons contain detailed instructions for the teacher, they can be used by a person with little experience. More experienced teachers will be able to use these same lessons as models for developing additional lessons of their own.

The unique feature of the program is that it solves the problem of providing meaningful activities or experiences in lieu of audio-visual aids, which most small groups and most small parishes cannot afford. In many instances it has been found that these activities have proven more effective than the audio-visuals they were intended to replace.

ABOUT THE AUTHOR

 Richard J. Reichert, Executive Director of the Appleton, Wisconsin, Catholic Education Council, is a graduate in English and Education with an MA in History from the University of Notre Dame, and an MA in Religious Education from Loyola University. He has taught both high school and college and is the author of a number of articles which have appeared in such scholarly journals as *Review for Religious* and *Living Light*.

CONTENTS

CONTENTS

PROGRAM FORMAT

I. INTRODUCTION

In the eight sessions described in the following pages you will meet with students in a home (or informally in a classroom). Each session is designed to last approximately two hours. However, you may shorten it at your discretion.

II. FORMAT OF THE SESSIONS

Introductory Activity (10 minutes)

In this section you will ask the students to engage in an activity designed to stimulate interest in the topic under discussion, or to illustrate a point you wish to make during the discussion. Occasionally props or other materials will be used in the introductory activity.

Student Reaction (15 minutes)

After the activity has been completed you will ask for reactions. These may vary widely from amusement to anger, but all reactions should be as honest as possible.

Instruction (15 minutes)

After students have had a chance to react to the activity, you will be expected to summarize these reactions, looking for trends or patterns common to most of the students (e.g., all felt anger). At this point you will speak rather directly about the topic under discussion, giving your own convictions (and those of the Church if it is a doctrinal topic). An outline for this instruction will be provided as an aid if you feel you want one.

Questions (15 minutes)

At this point you should ask students to react to you or what you have presented, either by way of question or objection. They should be encouraged to do this as candidly as possible, and you should attempt to respond with equal candor. Your goal is to enlighten rather than indoctrinate.

Break (10-15 minutes)

This is intended to give the students a chance to move around and relax a little. If you or the group plans to serve refreshments, such as soft drinks, this would be the logical place. Also you and the other adult leader may wish to leave the room at this point to evaluate how the session is going so far in case you want to alter your approach.

Second Activity (10 minutes)

This second activity is intended to refocus the attention of the group after the break, and like the first activity it should reinforce the topic under discussion.

Student Reaction/General Discussion (open-ended)

Students are again invited to give honest reactions to the activity. After you summarize these experiences as before, you should initiate a general discussion of the topic with the goal of arriving at some type of group consensus. To stimulate discussion you can ask questions, encourage others to participate and give your own observations . . . without dominating the discussion, however.

This discussion should last until a consensus has been reached, or until the topic no longer sustains interest.

(During this general discussion, students may end up on an entirely different topic. As long as they are sincerely interested in the new topic, you need not force them back to the planned topic.)

III. GENERAL DESCRIPTION OF THE TOPICS FOR THE EIGHT SESSIONS

Respect

Under the broad topic of respect you will explore the basic elements of all healthy human relationships: mutual respect which leads to mutual trust, which in turn leads to mutual cooperation and finally ends in mutual affection. On the other hand, you will attempt to trace the results of a relationship which begins with disrespect: distrust, anger, active antagonism, hatred.

At the same time you will ask the students to examine their own relationships with others: parents, teachers, classmates, persons of the opposite sex, etc.

The insights gained in this session will play an important part in future sessions and you will want to be able to refer back to them.

Core Morality

We are using the word, morality, here to refer to those values and goals of people which most shape their decisions. You will attempt to have the students express their own personal "morality" and then attempt to form a synthesis which best expresses the entire group's common values and goals.

In the event that they leave out or contradict Christian values and goals, your task will be to point this out and challenge them to re-evaluate their own position (for example, in the matter of stealing).

Freedom

Freedom is the third element (besides respect and common values) in any productive group or society. The task in this session will be to wrestle with the dilemma of protecting the individual's freedom to do his own thing (within a group), while protecting the right of the group to its own survival.

Necessity for Dreaming

In this session, the goal is to develop in the group a sense
of vision, a capacity to dream together—or what you
might call in technical terms, a future orientation which
is both meaningful and hopeful.

This sense of common vision is the fourth element of any
group or society that wishes to survive (beyond the
accomplishment of some single task—e.g., volunteer
rescue workers band together only to achieve a particular
rescue and then disband).

In the first four sessions, as you can see, the theme has been to
explore the elements which can be found in any productive (or
happy) group: mutual respect, common values and goals,
personal freedom and a future orientation. In the next four
sessions we hope to relate these ideas to an examination of the
Church.

The Gospel Dream

In the fourth session the students discussed the idea of
vision or future orientation and hope. In this session you
want to present and discuss the kind of vision and hope
the Gospel presents to all mankind and compare it with
other kinds of visions man has developed. This session is
the core session from a catechetical point of view. The
question under discussion is: Does the Gospel give
meaning to the life of the human community? This must,
of course, be related to the life as the students are now
experiencing it, and in terms of the core morality they
expressed in an earlier session.

The Church

In this session you want to explore the question of the
Church. Does it possess those qualities we saw in the first
four sessions as the key elements for any successful group
or society? And more important, does it possess them in
ways that are meaningful to the students and not just in
an abstract or ideal way? Finally, in what ways do the
students feel the Church lacks any of these four
elements: mutual respect, common values, freedom and
vision?

The Mission of the Church

In this discussion we wish to ask the question: What is the relation of the Church to the rest of the human community? Is the Church an end in itself or is it a community with a mission? What is this mission? Is there any role in this mission for the students *now?*

Celebration—the Sacramental Life of the Church

For our purposes we will approach the sacraments as celebrations of various aspects of our life, as our life is enriched by Christ. Thus we will first discuss the role and nature of celebration in human life and then see how the Church practices celebration. We will deal primarily with Eucharist and Reconciliation (Penance).

11

HOW TO USE THE EXERCISES

I. PURPOSE OF THE EXERCISES
The exercises are designed to help the students *feel* and
experience the topic which you will be treating in a
particular lesson. As such they are similar to audio-visual
aids (movies, etc.) but can be more effective because they
allow for more involvement and participation by the students.

II. HOW TO INTRODUCE AN EXERCISE
When it is time to begin an exercise, explain that while it
has the appearance of a game, the exercise is intended to
help them discover something about themselves or about
how people get along together. Thus you must encourage
them to "put themselves into it" even though what they are
asked to do may at first glance appear silly or foolish.
Encourage them to keep track of how they *feel* (embarrassed,
angry, frustrated, etc.) when they begin to participate.

However, do not tell them ahead of time how they should
feel and do not explain in detail what you hope will take
place. Allow room for discovery. Explain that they might
not realize until afterwards what really took place during the
exercise.

Finally, explain that while the exercises have a serious
purpose, they should be enjoyed. Nothing painful or
embarrassing will happen.

Then you are ready to give the specific instructions for the
exercise.

III. HOW TO GET THE MOST OUT OF AN EXERCISE

If the exercise is successful, the students themselves will have had enough feelings and experiences during it that they can now discuss it and the related topic with interest. Your task is to draw these feelings and experiences out of them by questions, samples of which are included in the instructions for the exercise. Do not hesitate, however, to develop questions of your own. Also, you may want to use some of the questions provided at the end of each lesson. Never read such questions to the students. Instead prepare yourself ahead of time by remembering the kinds of questions you could ask and then "throw them out" whenever you think it necessary to stimulate discussion or focus on the topic.

Also, it is very important that you observe all the students carefully during the exercises, attempting to pick up their reactions, their feelings, their attitudes. When the exercise is over, you will want to recall these so the students can then discuss them. For example: Joe, I noticed that you appeared angry when Tom did such and such. Is that really how you felt? Could you explain why you felt that way?

Finally, avoid putting a person on the spot and embarrassing him. Your questions and actions must be as emotionally non-threatening as possible. Stress that there are no wrong answers involved in these exercises. If students begin to fear the exercises as embarrassing situations, the exercises will cease to be effective.

IV. SOME PRACTICAL TIPS

Always prepare whatever props you need ahead of time. Students will lose interest if you have to stop to find a piece of paper or some other item.

In many exercises you are asked to divide the group into smaller groups. Develop some simple way to do this, but do not divide them into the same groups each time. Mix them up. And avoid any indication that you are showing favorites when you divide them.

When an exercise is to be done in silence, as several are, stress the importance of this for the effectiveness of an exercise. Explain that while it may seem natural to want to laugh, they should try to refrain.

When an exercise has a time limit, stick to it. This is intended to heighten suspense and create competition. Announce how much time they have and then announce periodically how much time is left.

Whenever possible, both you and your partner should participate. This will help the students take the exercise seriously and avoid the impression that you are using them as "experiments."

Allow enough time between an exercise and the discussion for the students to settle down. This can usually be achieved simply by asking them to gather around in a group. By the time they have situated themselves on the floor or in chairs, you can begin your discussion.

Even if an exercise did not "work," it can still be an effective discussion starter. In such a case you can explain what you hoped to achieve and then start from there, asking for example why they felt it did not work in this case.

With freshmen, the competitive element of most exercises will be the most effective motivation. With sophomores and juniors, the element of self-discovery will be an effective motivation. Stress each element accordingly.

Remember that the exercises are intended as aids. Don't become so preoccupied with them that you forget the topic you want to bring to the students' attention. On the other hand, don't force the topic on them prematurely. If the exercise generates sufficient interest in another direction, allow them to pursue it.

Your formal instruction should flow as naturally as possible from the discussion. Don't stop everything and say: "Now we are going to have a lesson."

The format for each meeting is not sacred; at your discretion and based on the needs of your group, you may wish to spend more time on one part than another, drop an exercise, expand the meeting, shorten or skip the break period, etc. The format, therefore, is a guideline; the success of a session will not depend on following it perfectly.

The best preparation for these exercises and meetings, and therefore the best teacher training is for the teachers to actually do the exercises together before they do them with the students. This is best done if the person responsible for teacher training assembles the teachers and leads them through a particular session before the teachers lead the students. Based on this experience, each teacher can then adapt the session to his own purposes.

CHARACTER SKETCHES OF THE ADOLESCENT PERSONALITY

I. INTRODUCTION

What follows are brief descriptions of some of the chief characteristics of the freshman, sophomore and junior boy and girl. You'll note that I continually warn you that these are generalizations that should be applied to individuals only with prudence.

These descriptions will probably support your own experiences with adolescents and will perhaps recall to mind some ideas you have forgotten. In this sense they should provide you with a general background of information. Never forget, however, that the key principle in relating to youth is to attempt as much as possible to treat them as the unique individuals they are—and are struggling to become. While the descriptions of the various age groups are valid, do not use them to categorize the youth with whom you are working.

Finally, your common sense and your own experience tell you that two principles are crucial in working with youth:

1. Sincere praise, encouragement and respect do more than anything else to help the youth develop a unique and healthy adult personality.

2. Never hesitate to state clearly and directly your own convictions, even when these contradict those of the youth. However, never demand that they conform to your convictions except in matters where you are certain grave personal harm would occur to them or others if they refused.

WARNING: THESE ARE GENERALIZATIONS. APPLY THEM WITH PRUDENCE TO INDIVIDUALS.

II. CHARACTER SKETCH OF THE FRESHMAN BOY

External Characteristics

He is self-conscious about his physical build and appearance. If *he* feels he is too fat, too thin, too short or too tall in comparison to others, it will inhibit his willingness to get up in front of others.

Despite bravado, he is generally shy around girls. He will tend to be very logical if you get him into a discussion, but he prefers action to discussion. He has a lot of physical energy which is manifested in overreaction in humorous situations and in spontaneous bursts of "roughhouse" or similar activities.

While some are courteous, freshman boys as a group tend to lack refinement in feelings. Due to sporadic bursts of growth they are extremely awkward and uneasy. They are not sympathetic or merciful, can find humor in others' misfortune or embarrassment. But they tend to be very just, believe strongly in fair play and will accept discipline when they feel it is in keeping with their "crime."

Because they still lack any strong sense of "self" they find much support in groups or gangs. Individually they are quite insecure and will seek advice, will often be polite and cooperative. In a group or gang, they will apparently contradict themselves and act cruelly or discourteously. In such situations "divide and conquer," or win the leader to "your side." Others will follow an individual's lead quickly.

Some Psychological Motivations at Work

Because he still lacks an "inner self-image" the freshman boy is prone to test himself in physical ways against others—strength, athletic skill, appearance—and in other forms of "contests" of bravery and intelligence. He is a "slave" to the approval or disapproval of his peers, especially those he admires.

He is definitely rejecting his childhood qualities which made him appealing—willing dependence, spontaneity, candidness—and replacing them with independence, self-direction, caution and inhibitiveness.

As a result he "leaves home" psychologically because home means childhood. Instead he seeks peer companionship, freedom to move about the "world," to come and go when and where he pleases.

Because he is caught between childhood and a more mature self-image, he sometimes fluctuates between childish actions and more mature ones—which confuses both him and the adults who work with him.

Some Educational Implications

Avoid whatever would appear to be treating freshman boys like children. Also avoid setting yourself apart from them as a group in such a way that the group feels the need to oppose you.

Stress rules of fair play, be consistent in applying rules. Use competition and games or contests to illustrate a point, but do not make these so threatening or humiliating to the "loser" that you magnify their already keen self-consciousness. Seldom pit boys against girls at this age.

Compliment achievements, praise generously, but don't overreact to failures and misbehavior.

Set *very concrete goals* and outline, in detail, procedures for reaching them. Demand that they stay within the rules—once they agree to the justice of the rules.

WARNING: THESE ARE GENERALIZATIONS. APPLY THEM WITH PRUDENCE TO INDIVIDUALS.

III. CHARACTER SKETCH OF THE FRESHMAN GIRL

External Characteristics
She is physically more advanced than the freshman boy and has already begun to form a self-image. It is largely based, however, on her physical appearance about which she is extremely self-conscious. The homely, fat or skinny girl will be very self-conscious and often try to compensate by withdrawal or by bizarre behavior.

She is sensitive and is easily hurt or pleased by others' reactions. She is dependent upon the approval of others and thus is prone to fads and current "popularity" gimmicks: She will be up on music, TV and movie stars, singers, etc.

She is much more interested in friendship and personal relationships than the boy her age. More interested in people than things.

At the same time, she is usually beginning to experience the "negative period" which we will describe in the sophomore character sketch. Hence she can be moody, depressed, generally disagreeable and critical.

Some Psychological Motivations at Work
She has usually outgrown childhood qualities but has not developed firm adult patterns of emotional behavior or an adult self-image. So she feels quite insecure, especially if she is not pleased with her external appearance. She seeks support in close friends—and prefers their companionship to that of parents or other family members.

She is more interested in boy-girl relationships than her male counterpart, but usually rejects the freshman boy as too immature. Because she is too young for the older boys, she often despairs of her chances to ever have a boyfriend.

She feels her emotions keenly and often reacts without restraint, which accounts for very unpredictable behavior. Tears one minute and laughter the next. Because she knows she can be easily and deeply hurt by rejection, she is quite guarded in a peer group.

Some Educational Implications
She reacts very well to kindness, praise, trust—being treated as an adult woman. She enjoys games and contests, provided they will not draw attention to what she considers her real weaknesses—e.g., overweight, poor complexion, etc.

She can discuss more readily than freshmen boys, but would prefer doing something to just talking. She is very impressionable (and critical)—will react very well to sincerity and be merciless to the phony.

Like her male counterpart, she prefers very concrete projects with concrete goals and well-outlined procedures. She will respond to adult leadership, provided it safeguards her sense of freedom and maturity.

WARNING: THESE ARE GENERALIZATIONS. APPLY THEM WITH PRUDENCE TO INDIVIDUALS.

IV. CHARACTER SKETCH OF THE SOPHOMORE BOY

External Characteristics
Tends to be very negative and critical of everyone and everything. Nothing can sustain his interest or loyalty for long. He is bored.

Tends to plunge into activities like sports or hobbies to relieve his boredom, but often loses interest in a short time. Leaves many "projects" only half finished. Unfortunately, in his effort to find relief from his boredom, he can often seek socially undesirable outlets. He will experiment in drinking and possibly in drugs.

Has little confidence in parents or most adults since they don't seem to "understand" and they can't help him find the meaning in life he is searching for. Thus he will be either indifferent to adults or actively critical and "bitchy."

Can be physically listless, "lazy," inactive. Thus he is a complete bundle of contradictions. Hyperactive but never completes anything. Very listless in the midst of all kinds of diversions and possible activities that formerly interested him.

He is often very unkempt and his room is a mess. Order has no value just now.

Some Psychological Motivations at Work
He is entering into the first or preliminary phase of adult maturity. But it takes the form of disenchantment with all that previously had meaning for him. Only after he has been "purged" of childhood meanings, can he discover old values in a new way and on a deeper level. Thus this period is very painful, full of "nothing," and creates moods of deep depression, loneliness, indifference to persons and things around him. He can be hard to live with.

He may pick up some bad habits—drinking, vandalism, etc.—as attempts to cope with his boredom and find some "excitement," but usually he outgrows quickly as he enters the next phase of growth, described in the next sketch.

His lashing out at parents and adults in general is based on frustration and does not indicate in most instances a real aversion to them. They are scapegoats for his own very real suffering at this stage.

Some Educational Implications
Don't overreact to his moods and unseemly behavior.

When he is interested in something, encourage him, but don't become disappointed when he loses interest, often within a short time after he began. (Basements are filled with guitars, drums and other projects at this period.)

He will not respond to reason, so logical arguments have little effect on him. The only way to reach him is through providing experiences for him—and by communicating a general acceptance of him despite his actions or lack of actions. He needs support at this stage, not advice.

Despite appearances, he is learning a great deal in this stage. However, most of it is negative in form. He is discovering the limitations within himself and in things that formerly had great importance to him—including parents. This is a necessary stage for building authentic and realistic values in the next stage of growth.

While we have described his negative qualities, the boy in this stage is not constantly displaying these qualities. At many times he will be quite agreeable, friendly, and cooperative.

WARNING: THESE ARE GENERALIZATIONS. APPLY THEM WITH PRUDENCE TO INDIVIDUALS.

V. CHARACTER SKETCH OF THE SOPHOMORE GIRL

External Characteristics
The sophomore girl will share many of the negative characteristics of the sophomore boy. However, because she is more likely to have begun this negative stage in her freshman year, she is often emerging from it during her sophomore year.

At any rate, she, like the boy, will attempt to find meaning in life and relief from boredom by testing out new kinds of behavior—anything from dying her hair to taking up knitting (or running away from home). Usually maintains personal neatness, but her room will often be a disaster area.

She is very susceptible to being hurt, easily depressed, can react with deep feelings of anger. In general the girl always feels more keenly and intensely than the boy. Thus she tends to move to the next stage more quickly, but pays for it by experiencing this negative stage more intensely.

Some Psychological Motivations at Work
In general these are the same as those the boy is experiencing—rejection of all past values and meanings, which have proven superficial, and a frustrating search for new and deeper meanings to life.

Remember, however, that most girls are a year or so ahead of the boy in emotional and physical development. So what we say about the sophomore boy may be true for the freshman girl. What we say about the junior boy may be true for the sophomore girl. Because girls feel more deeply, they can also be more cruel in what they say and do when experiencing the pain and frustration of this period.

Some Educational Implications
As in the case of the boys, your best approach to help them grow is to encourage them in their current interest and not be disappointed when they discontinue a project when it is half finished.

Avoid direct confrontation and logical debate. Manifest disapproval at their outbursts of anger, disrespect, etc., but don't let yourself become emotional or overreact.

Allow them the freedom to test out various forms of behavior—without shirking your adult responsibility to protect them from what would permanently be damaging to health or moral character.

Just as in the case of the sophomore boy, they are learning—but it is negative. They are learning what they and things lack, rather than what they possess.

WARNING: THESE ARE GENERALIZATIONS. APPLY THEM WITH CAUTION TO INDIVIDUALS.

VI. CHARACTER SKETCH OF THE JUNIOR BOY AND GIRL

External Characteristics
By now most boys have caught up with girls in physical development and have also become their emotional equals—although the girl tends to remain more sensitive and continues to feel things more deeply than boys.

While some boys and girls will continue to experience some of the negative characteristics described in the sophomore stage, most juniors are beginning to manifest characteristics which will continue well into their twenties.

They become idealistic. They become keenly interested in absolutes like beauty, justice, peace, truth. They become keenly interested in personal relationships and most fall in love for the first time—a love that is idealistic and romantic.

Many will write poetry or seek other ways to express their newfound feelings and insights into life and themselves.

They will begin to test out their interior qualities—seek an identity based on their real qualities and not just on externals. They begin to have a future orientation for the first time, one that usually centers around college for boys and marriage for girls.

They will be highly critical of pat answers to serious problems—like morality, religion, social justice—but will often themselves present only simplistic "absolute" answers to these problems themselves. They will succeed in solving problems all past generations failed to solve. They don't have much patience with tradition. They have a keen sense of personal freedom and seek expressions of independence, and they will often frighten parents by asking for freedoms which are not justified by their experience or their ability to assume responsibility.

Psychological Motivations at Work

This accounts for their new enthusiasm for life, a sudden maturity of interests, but also accounts for their criticism of older generations (who have lost their idealism and replaced it with prudence and "compromise") and they will often accuse parents and other adults of selling out to the "establishment" for the sake of financial security.

Note: This kind of criticism can be painful to parents and other adults for two reasons: It often contains a kernel of truth; it is often unfair and seems to indicate a lack of appreciation for all the sacrifices parents and other adults have made in behalf of the youth.

Because juniors begin to realize just how differently they view the world in comparison to their parents' approach to life, the youth become convinced that there is a real lack of understanding between them and parents and often despair of ever bridging the gap.

Educational Implications

Encourage their idealism, their creative expression, appeal to their newfound enthusiasm and optimism.

Attempt to provide practical outlets for this idealism and enthusiasm. If it remains theory and is never tested by the practical obstacles life presents, they never will achieve the balance between idealism and reality.

Seek out common ground, areas in which you can agree wholeheartedly, in order to help break down their idea that there is an unbridgeable gap between them and adults.

In areas where you do not agree, avoid debate. Rather, state your convictions clearly without demanding that they accept them—and make sure you back up your convictions with practical action (e.g., don't talk about your convictions about social justice unless you can demonstrate these convictions by the way you act). At the same time, encourage them to explain in detail their own convictions and seek for clarifications when there seems to be a contradiction. However, your questions have to be motivated by interest and a desire to understand them, not be a desire to "prove they are wrong." In other words, help them think through their rather generalized and idealistic solutions. In doing so they themselves will often discover the contradictions or impractical nature of some of their ideas. Never push them into a situation where you can then say, "I told you so." And don't appeal to answers like "that's how man has always acted." Most arguments are ineffective, especially those based on tradition.

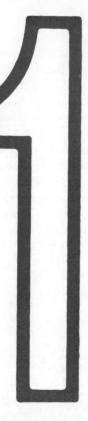

RESPECT

The main goal of this session is to help the students experience the nature and role of respect in their relations with others. We prefer this term (respect) to others like charity and friendship because the latter words are often overworked and are usually reserved for special relationships with just a few people.

Respect is more basic and more within our day-to-day experiences. It forms the foundation for other relationships—and this is what we would like to get across to the students.

I. BEGINNING EXERCISE

This first exercise is designed to give the students an experience of what it is to be respected and/or disrespected.

Instructions:

    1. Prepare ahead of time a number of paper hats with one of the following titles on each of them:

a. drunk
b. Negro militant
c. name of famous athlete
d. conceited boy (or girl)
e. nun
f. priest
g. policeman
h. good friend
 i. unfair teacher
 j. loudmouth

Note: You may make a variation on this list to suit your local situation.

2. Ask the group to sit in a circle facing each other. Tell them that each person will receive a hat which will describe the kind of person he or she represents. NO ONE SHOULD LOOK AT HIS OWN HAT, BUT HE MAY LOOK AT THOSE OF THE OTHERS.

Then we will assume we are together at a party. We should react to each person as we feel we would honestly react if they were the person the sign says. E.g., if the person represented would anger you, act angry; if the person represented is someone you would like, act friendly, etc. However, do not tell the other person directly "who they are." They must try to guess based on the reactions of others. You likewise must try to guess whom you are representing.

3. After you have placed a hat on each person, ask the students to greet each other in the way they would if they were actually facing the kind of person the hat describes—but in such a way as to not let the other person know whom he or she represents. Each person, based on the kinds of greetings he receives from others, attempts to guess what title he has on his own hat.

4. After about five minutes—or until everyone has had a chance to interreact with three or four people, ask them to sit down and have each member of the group tell whom they think they are representing. Then allow them to look at their own hats.

II. STUDENT REACTION

After everyone has found out "who he is" you can explain that you were trying to help them experience what it is like to be respected or disrespected when you don't know why. Then you can seek their own reactions to the experience by some of the following questions:

1. Did you find it hard to give an honest reaction? Did you perhaps feel a little embarrassed or silly?

2. If people were reacting to you with disrespect, did you find it hard to be friendly to them? How did it feel if most people were unfriendly to you? Did it hurt?

3. If people were reacting to you in a friendly way, did you find it hard to be unfriendly even though the person represented was one with whom you would not ordinarily be friendly? How did it feel when most people were friendly to you? Did you like it?

4. How did you feel not knowing whom you represented— uneasy, amused, curious? If you guessed who you were, what were some of the clues?

After you feel the students have had sufficient time to give their reactions, you can move into the instruction portion.

III. INSTRUCTION AND DISCUSSION

(The outline for the formal instruction and the discussion questions are found at the end of the lesson.)

BREAK PERIOD

IV. SECOND EXERCISE

Like the first exercise, this is intended to help the students experience feelings of respect and disrespect and how these affect our relations with others. The main difference is that this will be more a group than an individual experience.

Instructions:

1. Divide the group into two equal groups, with one adult leader in each half.

2. Group A should then go to a separate room or at least out of hearing of Group B.

3. Group A is informed that when it comes back into the room, every member of the group is to, in some nonverbal way (a sneer, sticking out the tongue, etc.), manifest rejection and disrespect of Group B. They can walk up to different members of Group B and should continue to show this disrespect until the leader signals to stop. Encourage them to "feel mean" and not laugh, even though it seems humorous.

4. Meanwhile, Group B should be instructed that Group A is voting on them and will either come back showing approval or rejection. In either case, however, Group B should show respect and approval of Group A in some nonverbal way; for example, by offering to shake hands, smiling, attempting to put their arm around their shoulders, etc. They should be encouraged to be sincere about their effort and not start giggling, even if it seems funny.

5. When the two groups come back together, this display of rejection by Group A and approval by Group B should continue for a minute or more. It should be prolonged, if possible, for about two minutes, but should be stopped if people all get the giggles and can't stop laughing.

V. STUDENT REACTION AND DISCUSSION

Once the leader of Group A calls time, then you should discuss the following: (You can word the questions any way you see fit.)

1. For Group A—When you saw that Group B was showing their approval of you, did you find it hard to keep rejecting them? Did it help to be in a group, knowing you were all doing the same thing?

2. For Group B—Did you feel nervous about being voted on? Did you find any strength in the fact that you were in a group and not just alone?

3. For Group B—Once you saw that Group A rejected you, did you find it hard to continue to show respect? Did you feel the desire to return like for like, that is, begin to show rejection to them? Would you have done so if some others in the group began to show rejection too? Did you feel closer to your group when you realized that the whole group was in it together?

VI. ALTERNATE SECOND EXERCISE

Instructions:

Prepare ahead of time as many small slips of paper as you have persons in the group. On half of these slips write the word "friendly," on the other slips write the word "unfriendly." Fold the slips so the word is not visible.

Distribute one slip to each person in the group including yourself and the other adult leader. Each person may look at his slip, but he should tell no one what it says.

Now explain that we are all members of an imaginary committee that has been asked to decide upon a new name for the school newspaper (or a new name for the school teams). Everyone should try to give suggestions and we'll decide as a group upon the best ideas. *However,* as we work together, each person should act in the way described on his slip of paper, no matter how others act.

Allow about five minutes—or longer if the students get interested —in trying to decide upon a name. Then you can begin asking some of the following questions:

1. Based on how people were acting as we tried to decide upon a name, can we divide the group into two kinds of people? Whom would you put in each group?

2. If you were one of the "friendly" ones, did you find yourself beginning to get closer to other friendly people and ignoring others less friendly?

3. If you were an unfriendly person, did you find support from others who seemed to be acting the same way as you? Did you find yourself becoming closer to them? Did you find it hard being unfriendly to those who were trying to be friendly?

4. Have you ever been in groups in which this kind of thing happened?

VII. STUDENT REACTION

By the means of the above questions and others you may develop, encourage the students to continue to explore how it feels to respect and disrespect people and how it feels to be respected or disrespected. Attempt to have them make application in their own situations at home, at school, in other activities. Help them draw some conclusions about the effects of respect and disrespect in their relations with others.

INSTRUCTION ON RESPECT

(Note to adult leader: *The outline below is intended as a sample outline on the topic. To be effective, it must be developed and adapted by you, that is, put into your own words and style, and filled out with sufficient examples taken from your own and the students' experience.*)

Introduction

In the activity we just finished we tried to demonstrate what it feels like to have people respect us and disrespect us and to get some idea of the kind of reaction these feelings promote in us. Now we'd like to spend just a few minutes examining a little more closely the idea of respect. You can react to my comments when I finish.

Definition

When we talk about respect in this context we are talking about a very basic and frequent attitude one person has toward another. It might be called a "gut" feeling, as opposed to some surface action like good manners. And it is habitual rather than occasional.

So by respect we mean that gut feeling we have toward others which makes us assume they are good people and deserve fair treatment from us.

This kind of "good attitude" toward others is like a positive prejudice. We give other persons the benefit of the doubt even though we have no real proof that they are worthwhile. You might call it a kind of basic optimism about the people which enables us to like them before we really have a reason to. Respect is what makes us say that someone is a "good guy" before we have any real reason to say it, other than that someone happens to be a human being.

So respect in the way we mean it is a basic good attitude toward men in general, and we feel this way about the individuals we meet, regardless of their age, how they look, how they dress, etc.

The opposite of respect is, of course, disrespect. It is a basic gut feeling toward mankind which makes us reject people and turn them off before we have a real reason to do so. We decide they are no good in a kind of gut way, without any proof. Disrespect, like respect, is a kind of habitual attitude toward individuals or groups, and so is a kind of negative prejudice.

Respect at Work

When respect is the most basic attitude we have toward other people in general, then we are actually applying the golden rule in its most basic form. For each of us wants other people to like us, or at least give us a chance. No one wants to be judged a **35** loser without being given a chance. So to respect others is really to treat them the way we want others to treat us.

When two people start out by having this basic attitude of respect toward each other—we can feel it when someone respects us—you have the foundation for a friendship. On the other hand, if one person shows basic disrespect for the other, they don't have a chance of becoming friends until that attitude of disrespect changes into respect.

When two people know they respect each other, they feel safe with each other, that is, they don't have to always worry about what the other is thinking. So respect results in *trust*, which in turn leads to *communication*. This is not automatic. You don't completely trust someone all at once, and you don't start out all at once with really good communication. You have to work at trust and communication. But, you can't even get started at these until you have a mutual respect for each other.

After people learn to trust and communicate with each other, they begin to cooperate with each other, and help each other with their mutual problems. There is no real cooperation between people until there is some basic trust and communication. And there is no basic trust and communication until there is some basic respect for each other.

The Main Point

The main point we are trying to make is that there can be no really united group of people—family, school group or nation, unless there is a basic foundation of mutual respect for one another. The elements of any friendly relationship then are these:

a. a basic attitude of *respect* as the starting point—most relationships never get to this point because either we or the other guy fails to have this main ingredient, respect for the other.

b. this respect makes us feel safe, so we can *trust* and communicate with the other person.

c. a willingness to help the other when we learn what the other needs.

d. friendship usually results when people begin helping each other with their problems.

Some Applications of the Approach to Respect

a. Most problems between parents and high school students seem to stem from the failure of parents to *show* this respect to their children (they keep treating them as if they were babies, which is a lack of respect); or the teen fails to show this respect for his parents, usually by ignoring them or not listening to them.

b. Most people feel lonely in high school and at the same time feel that most of their fellow students don't really respect them. This may or may not be true, but as long as they *feel* that way, they are afraid to trust their classmates, so they remain out of touch with them.

c. Most hang-ups between people in authority and those under them, e.g., teachers and students, start when one or the other of these groups fails to show basic respect.

d. This lack of fundamental respect seems to be at the basis of black-white race relations, international problems, etc.

e. In areas like dating (boy-girl relations) this element of mutual respect is the crucial factor for the beginning of a friendship. If a boy, for example, lacks basic respect for girls, it comes through, and the girls usually turn him off.

Conclusion

The main point is: If individuals, groups and society at large are going to develop friendly relations and a peaceful, happy, mutually helpful relationship, they have to start with this kind of basic respect.

Our group is a kind of little "world." We will become a very friendly and productive, mutually helpful group only to the degree that we are able to start with this respect for persons in the group.

RESPECT

TH GRADE GROUPS

1   If a person doesn't respect you, do you think he can fake it, or can you usually tell that he doesn't? How? What are some clues you notice when a person does respect you?

2   Do you think most kids in your school (or class) respect each other in the way described? Do most boys respect the girls (girls answer first)? Do you think most girls respect the boys (boys answer first)? How do they show their respect or disrespect?

3   Often we hear that students in junior high school have very little respect for older people, for example, on the street, in stores, at the movies, etc. We hear that they are usually rude, give smart answers when spoken to, will insult them for no reason. Do you think this is true?

a) If you think it is true, why do you think they act that way?

b) If you think it is not true, why do people still think kids are that way?

4 Do you think most teachers respect the students at your school? Do most kids respect the teachers? How do students or teachers show their respect or disrespect?

5 Judging from your own friends, do you think you trust them because they show this respect to you?

6 Do you know any real loners, kids whom no one seems to respect and who are usually made fun of or teased by others? Why do people act that way toward them? Can you think of anything worse than being laughed at, really laughed at, by your classmates?

7 When parents and high school children aren't getting along, do you think lack of respect is the basis for it? Do parents usually respect their children or do they usually treat them as babies—a form of disrespect? What are some ways kids show disrespect to their parents?

8 There is usually a lot of rivalry between schools in things like athletics. In sports is this rivalry based on disrespect for kids in other schools or just healthy competition or both? Do most kids respect the kids who go to a rival school?

9 Why is it that when a junior high school student is alone he usually seems more respectful to others, for example, older people, than when he or she is in a large group? From your experience is this true?

10 Can you think of someone in your school whom you usually treat with disrespect (don't use names)? Why do you think you act that way? What do you think would happen if you began to show this general respect we've been talking about? Can you think of anyone whom you didn't like at first but later became good friends with?

Q U E S T I O N S

RESPECT

10

TH GRADE GROUPS

1 Do you think seniors at your school respect tenth grade students in the way we've described? If not, why not? How do they show their respect or lack of respect?

2 Do tenth grade boys usually respect or disrespect girls? (Girls answer.) How do they show it or why do you feel that way? Do tenth grade girls usually respect or disrespect the boys in their class? (Boys answer.) What makes you feel that way?

Boys: Do you agree with the girls on what they said?
Girls: Do you agree with the boys on what they said?

3 Does this become a problem with dating, going to dances, etc.?

4 Often we hear that high school students don't respect older people, for example, on the street, in stores, at movies, etc. We hear that they are rude, make smart remarks when spoken to, make fun of others with insults, vulgarities, etc.

Is this true in your opinion? If so, why do you think they act that way? If you don't think it is generally true, why do people say that it is?

5 Do you think that in most families parents and their high school children respect, trust and communicate with each other? If not, what's the problem? Why don't kids respect their parents and why do parents treat kids like babies, which is a form of disrespect?

6 Do you know any kids at your school who have been really cut off by the group and are generally treated with disrespect? Why? Do you think your classmates in general respect or disrespect each other?

7 Since we are talking about a gut feeling that is rather habitual, can you fake respect? Can you really hide it when you don't respect someone?

8 From your experience, do you think you usually show respect to strangers when you are alone, but when you are in a group, say downtown, you are more apt to show disrespect to strangers? Why?

9 Do you think adults in general respect or disrespect high school students? Do you think high school students in general respect or disrespect adults? Can you give reasons for your answers?

10 When a person acts disrespectfully to others, say by being rude, insulting, etc., can it often come more from fear and embarrassment than from actual disrespect for the other?

11 If you think there is a generation gap, do you think lack of respect is the cause or just the result?

Q
U
E
S
T
I
O
N
S

RESPECT

TH GRADE GROUPS

1 Is it realistic to expect someone to have this general respect for everyone he or she meets? Can you really call it a habit or a kind of fixed attitude toward people, or is it more a response you feel after you get to know them?

2 Girls: Do most junior and senior boys respect or disrespect girls? Why do you feel that way? Why do you think they feel that way?

Boys: Do you agree or disagree with the girls?

Boys: Do most junior and senior girls respect or disrespect boys? Why do you feel that way? Why do you think they feel that way?

Girls: Do you agree or disagree with the boys' comments?

3 If you feel there is a generation gap in general, or at least one within your own family, is it based on a failure to respect each other, or does disrespect come as a result of the generation gap?

4 In general, do you think high school juniors respect or disrespect adults, for example, parents and teachers? Why do you feel that way? Do you think adults in general respect or disrespect high school students? Why would they feel that way?

5 Why do you think we all want and need the respect of others? Can you think of anything worse than not being respected by people, for example, the kids in your class?

6 Is this gut-level disrespect at the root of racial prejudice? **43**
Is there any real cure for this kind of prejudice?

7 What do you think your school, or society at large would be like if most people really did have this gut-level feeling of respect for each other? What kind of problems would disappear from your school, for example? Can you think of any new problems that might come about if people respected each other? Can you respect someone too much?

8 Rugged individualism, the strong, silent loner, the self-reliant character, for example, the Steve McQueen or James Bond type, is often held up as an ideal personality in our society. Is this realistic? Or is it an escape? Does this type of person usually respect or disrespect others? Can this type ever make friends? Can he get along without them? Can any of us ever get along without friends?

2

CORE MORALITY

The goal of the session is to give the students some insight into the true nature and role of morality in society. This is achieved by helping them to evaluate their own moral values and compare them with those of others in the group.

Ultimately, it is hoped that the group would come to some basic agreement on values; that is, develop a core morality which the whole group could accept.

Note: In the exercises in this session, there is no "correct" ordering of the values. So stress that the group is free to order them any way it wants to. You do not want to give the impression that you have the answer and want them to arrive at it. In the formal instruction and discussion you can challenge them if they seem to have warped ideas of morality.

I. BEGINNING EXERCISE

The purpose of this exercise is to get the students to think through their own moral standards and compare them with those of others. This is *not* a competitive exercise, so each student has a right to defend his own position.

Instructions:

1. Obtain a set of seven slips of paper or cards for each person in the group.

2. Write on each card one of the following:

    Card 1. Whatever causes me to feel physical pain

    Card 2. Whatever causes me to feel mental/emotional pain

    Card 3. Whatever causes damage or loss to my property

    Card 4. Whatever causes me to be ignorant or phony

    Card 5. Whatever takes away my freedom to decide my future

    Card 6. Whatever causes me to lose my reputation and friendship with others

    Card 7. Whatever causes me to lose my own self-respect

3. When each person has been given a set of cards, ask each person to arrange the cards in such a way that the top card is the worst thing a person could do to him, the second card is the second worst thing a person could do to him, etc., until he has arranged all seven cards in order of "worst thing."

    Give about five minutes or as long as it takes, stressing that it is a personal matter, not a test.

4. When everyone has his cards arranged, then ask each person to put his top card on the table (or in the center of the floor). These can then be shuffled so no one knows what the others have put in. Then do the same with the

second, third, etc., until you have seven piles of cards in order.

5. Now, in each pile determine if there is any kind of consensus or majority, e.g., most cards in the first pile have physical pain on them.

In this way, draw up a list which the majority of the group has agreed upon.

II. STUDENT REACTION

Using this list as the starting point, now you can discuss together why different people ordered the cards the way they did.

III. INSTRUCTION AND DISCUSSION

(The outline for the formal instruction and discussion questions are found at the end of the lesson.)

BREAK PERIOD

IV. SECOND EXERCISE

The purpose of this exercise is similar to that of the first, but should make the question of core morality more concrete.

Instructions:

1. Prepare ahead of time five small signs on slips of paper:

   a. thief
   b. pornographer
   c. pusher

d. cheat

e. slanderer

On five other slips write:

a. to juvenile officer for arrest

b. expulsion from school

c. two weeks' suspension

d. probation

e. stern verbal correction

2. Ask for five volunteers to represent culprits. Give each person one of the slips indicating a "criminal." One of the adult leaders may wish to volunteer.

3. The rest of the group is to act as the school's discipline board. Explain that these five people have been sent to you because they were caught involved in the following activities at school:

a. the thief was stealing the principal's hub caps

b. the pornographer was selling obscene pictures to little kids

c. the pusher was selling pot in the cafeteria

d. the cheat was caught copying during a driver's ed test

e. the slanderer was accusing an innocent girl of sleeping with several boys (this can be restated in other words)

The discipline board must give out a punishment to each person by giving each one of the slips indicating the punishment. Instruct them that they are free to stretch or ignore the law, using as their criteria their own convictions about what are the most and least serious acts. For example, they may decide the slanderer should be arrested and the thief given a warning, although the existing law would be just the opposite.

4. Have the culprits sit on the floor and the disciplinary board in chairs or some similar position of authority. The board should discuss each case and make its decisions in

a way the culprits can hear and follow the discussions, but the culprits should remain silent and not try to defend themselves.

V. STUDENT REACTION

After each person has been given his punishment by the board, you can begin the student reaction period with some of the following questions:

1. For the culprits: How did it feel to be a criminal? Did you think your punishment fitted your crime? What punishment did you think would be more fitting?

2. To members of the board: Did you agree with the punishments or just go along with the rest to maintain peace? If you did differ, how would you have distributed the punishments and why?

3. For everyone: Are the "crimes" mentioned realistic of some of the things that go one in schools? Did you think some more important or serious or common "crimes" than these should have been used as examples? What are they?

4. If the punishments did not in every case agree with what the law usually allows, can you think of other "crimes" many people commit that are not punishable by law? What are some?

From this, help guide the students to some conclusions about developing a core morality. It would be good to go back to the list drawn up in the first exercise and compare it with how the punishments were handed out and also to continue the discussion of that list to see how much real agreement you can arrive at concerning a core morality of values.

INSTRUCTION ON CORE MORALITY

(Note to adult leader: *The outline below is intended as a sample outline on the topic. To be effective, it must be developed and adapted by you, that is, put into your own words and style, and filled out with sufficient examples taken from your own and the students' experiences.*)

Introduction

Last meeting we discussed the importance of mutual respect. Without this basic attitude of respect for others there is little sense in discussing what are right and wrong ways of treating one another. So this talk presumes you already see the need for respecting others, in the general way we talked about before.

Who Are We?

It is possible to get a pretty good idea of ourselves from the kinds of things we think are important and the kinds of things that make us unhappy.

Based on how you arranged the list of things that hurt a person, we can say that we are several things at once:

a. We are social, that is, we seem to be made to live in some kind of friendly, cooperative relationship with others. This seems to be the main thing about us. *We need each other to be happy.*

b. Because of this, our *reputation*—how others judge us— and our *self-respect*—how we judge ourselves—are very important. Without a good reputation and some good feelings toward ourselves, we really can't have friendly, cooperative relationships with others.

c. At the same time as we want to be on good terms with

others and cooperate with them, we also need very much to have some kind of personal control over our decisions: We need very much to be free to make choices which will shape our present and future relationships with others.

d. Finally, because we are physical, our relationships depend very much on our physical happiness—enough food, clothes, good health, etc. So anything we do that takes this kind of thing away at least indirectly makes it impossible to have good relationships.

What Is Morality?

Morality is not laws, restrictions and commands *added* onto life. Morality flows out of life itself; it is our conscious effort to *become* what man is intended to be. Consequently, it is basically positive. It is doing those things man, by his very nature, is intended to do. Only by flipping the coin does it become negative: avoiding those things that prevent man from being and becoming what he is supposed to be.

The key of all morality, therefore, is knowing what man is supposed to *become*. What is man supposed to be? That's the real question.

Based on your list of what hurts a man, we are suggesting that man is primarily intended to learn how to live together in a friendly, cooperative way. *Friendship* itself is in a sense what a man is intended to experience.

So morality is really doing whatever helps us and others become friends. To be immoral is to destroy either directly or indirectly whatever chance we ourselves and others have to live together in friendship and cooperation.

In that sense, it is obvious why some things have always been considered immoral or wrong:

a. ruining a guy's or girl's reputation by telling bad things about them

b. stealing, destroying property or hurting a person physically in other ways

c. being a phony—or forcing someone else to be phony

d. not giving the other guy a chance to make his own decisions either by using physical force, economic force or by keeping him ignorant (e.g., brain washing)

e. ignoring, turning off, ridiculing and mocking others because they don't meet our own standards (e.g., Negroes, unattractive, unintelligent, unathletic, old, etc.)

Role of Morality

As said last week, mutual respect is the basis for any successful group or society. Unless a group arrives at a common or core morality, though, it will not be able to function. Everyone may have good intentions, but there still won't be cooperation. So the second ingredient for any group or any society is to have some kind of rather clearly defined core morality, based on a common understanding of the nature and needs of man.

The list you just constructed would be an example of what we mean by a group's core morality.

Summary and Application

Morality isn't artificial.

It is simply doing whatever helps us become and allows others to become what man is supposed to become.

So it really isn't complicated and "legal," as we tend to think. It really depends on how well we understand that people are supposed to help each other rather than use each other. That people are supposed to be friends.

The real trick is being *honest with yourself*.

Too often we play "moral games," looking for excuses to keep doing what we *feel* is wrong.

CORE MORALITY

TH GRADE GROUPS

1   Do you think junior high school students can be good
    judges on what is good for them and for men in general,
    or do you think they need to be told what is right and
    wrong?

2   Do you think we can really judge right and wrong in
    terms of what helps us and others become friends and
    live in cooperation with each other? Do you think this
    would be a good guideline for junior high school
    students? If this isn't a good guide, what do you think
    would be one?

3   Do most junior high school students really care about what is right and wrong? Do they worry about doing the right thing? Are they often confused about what is the right thing? Can you give some examples of what confuses them?

4   If we used the guide of what helps us to become friends, then does this help us decide what would be wrong in regard to using our sexual powers?

5   Using the guideline of friendship, what do you think is the most "immoral" thing most high school students do?

6   In this same way, do you think adults are more "immoral" than teenagers? Why? What do adults do that is so "immoral" in terms of helping men to become friends?

7   Do you think there is a core morality at work in your school among high school students? Is it anything like the one we have been working out?

8   Do you think the kind of core morality we are talking about and trying to work out is much different from the kind of "right and wrong" that the Christians use to judge moral and immoral action?

9   What in your opinion, using friendship as the basis of our core morality, is the worst kind of thing young people do to adults? What is the worst kind of thing adults do to young people?

10   Do you think America has a core morality based on a common conviction of what man should become? What is it? What do you think most Americans think man should become?

CORE MORALITY

10

TH GRADE GROUPS

1. Can you agree that the best way to determine right and wrong is to first determine what mankind is supposed to become? If you don't agree, what do you think should be the base for a core morality?

2. Do you think people your age can be good judges of right and wrong? Do you think they care? Do you think they are confused about some things? What kind of decisions regarding right and wrong do you think give the most trouble to tenth grade students like yourselves?

3. If we used the criteria of what helps people to become friends with others as the basis of our core morality, what kind of sexual actions and experiences would be wrong for unmarried persons like yourselves?

4   Using this same criteria of friendship, what do you think
    is the worst deed high school students can do to each
    other? To their parents? In society at large, that is, to
    people they don't know and live with?

5   Do you think America has a clear idea of what is
    supposed to be? Does it have a core morality? Would you
    judge America as moral or immoral, using friendship as
    the basis?

6   Do you think there is a core morality at work in your
    school? What do you think it is?

7   Is this idea of core morality built on friendship much   **55**
    different from what you have always been taught is the
    morality that Christ taught his followers? If you think
    there is a difference, what do you think it is, in terms of
    what has been considered good and bad actions for a
    Christian?

8   Do you think most adults have a different idea of right
    and wrong from high school students? If you do, what is
    the cause of the difference? Do you think you could teach
    adults? Do you think adults and high school students
    could learn something from each other? What do you
    think they could teach high school students?

9   What makes things like racial prejudice immoral?

10 Can young people be honest when they sometimes say
    that they do bad things because they see adults doing
    them? Must kids always imitate adults, or are they free to
    act differently when they know it would be wrong to
    imitate them? For example, can a kid excuse himself for
    getting drunk because his dad gets loaded when he goes
    to a party?

CORE MORALITY

11 TH GRADE GROUPS

1 Do you agree that the best way to determine right and wrong is to first determine what mankind is supposed to become? If you don't agree, what do you think is the basis for a core morality? Or do you even think man should have a core morality? Is morality too personal and individual to come up with a moral code or a core morality?

2 Do you think most high school juniors and seniors can be good judges of what is good and bad for them—and others? Or do you think they still need advice and help from adults? What kind of moral decisions must high school juniors make that they find the most difficult and confusing?

3   If we used something like the idea that man is intended to learn how to live in friendship with all others, then what would make sexual activity among unmarried people wrong? Would the use of drugs be immoral? Would censorship of movies and TV be a problem for the government or a personal matter?

4   Does America have a core morality based on its idea of what man is supposed to be? If you think it does (or has several different ones) can you describe them? Do you agree in general with any of them or the most common one, if you think there is a most common one?

5   In your opinion, what is the most immoral thing high school students do to their fellow students? To their parents? To people they meet or work with in society but don't really know? To strangers?

6   On the other hand, what do you think is the most immoral thing adults do to high school students? To each other? To the people they work with? To society at large (e.g., unfair labor practices, etc.)?

7   Is the Christian morality you learned as a child pretty much the same thing we are talking about now when we talk about a morality based on the goal of friendship? Are the Ten Commandments much different from what we are talking about?

8   Would it help you if you felt that most people your age all share the same core morality? Do we depend pretty much on others to decide what is right and wrong? Do we need help from others to do the right thing once we decide?

9   There is a lot of criticism today by young people who say that adults are phony and hypocrites? Do you think most high school students are any less phony than adults or any less hypocritical when it comes to morality?

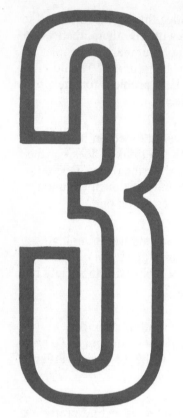

FREEDOM

The goal of the session is to help students experience the dilemma that exists when there is a conflict between individual and group freedom. At the same time it is intended to give students a better understanding of the true nature of freedom and its role in their lives.

I. BEGINNING EXERCISE

The purpose of this exercise is to demonstrate the nature of the conflict between the individual and group freedom, thus preparing the students for a discussion of this conflict as it exists in their own lives.

Instructions:

Before the group arrives, take an old deck of cards. Remove from it the heart suit and the spade suit. "Hide" in rather obvious places about the room 12 of the cards in each suit. Keep the king of hearts and the king of spades, however, to give later to a volunteer.

1. When you are ready to begin, ask for one volunteer. Then divide the remainder of the group into two teams, the heart team and the spade team.

2. Each team is to find its cards and arrange them in order, ace through king. The first team to gather and put all its cards in order wins; the losing team must furnish the refreshments the next meeting. (This should serve as a good motivating force for the teams, but if you feel it will not work in your group, decide upon some other "prize" which will add excitement to the game.)

3. Before they begin their search, explain that the volunteer has been given both the king of hearts and the king of spades. Hence, he holds the key to victory for each team.

   However, he is allowed to surrender only *one* card. If *he* gives up both cards, he alone must buy the refreshments for the next meeting. Stress that the volunteer is caught in a dilemma between his individual rights and group rights.

   So each group must attempt to persuade the volunteer to surrender the card they need, but at no time can they use force.

4. When everyone is aware of the "rules," have them begin their search and assembly process. Once one team wins, gather the group together and give a chance for reaction.

II. STUDENT REACTION

You can help students react to the exercise with some of the following questions:

1. Did you feel sympathetic with the volunteer or did you find yourself getting angry at him?

2. Did you feel an urge to use force when other things weren't working?

3. If your team lost, do you blame the volunteer or do you feel that you failed to persuade him properly? Did you think he was fair in his decision to give the card to the other team? Did your group respect the volunteer's freedom?

4. Did anyone feel the group was more important than the individual?

5. Have you ever experienced this kind of pull between freedoms in real-life situations?

III. INSTRUCTION AND DISCUSSION

(The outline for the formal instruction and discussion questions are found at the end of this lesson.)

BREAK PERIOD

IV. SECOND EXERCISE

The purpose of this exercise is to demonstrate the personal problem of freedom: We want freedom, but with it comes a responsibility to others. If we don't like responsibility, we tend to give up or misuse our freedom.

Instructions:

1. Using the same deck of cards as previously, give each person three cards.

2. Divide the group into two smaller groups and give them these instructions:

   a. They are not allowed to speak.

   b. Each group is to attempt to build a card house in which every person in the group uses all three of his cards.

   c. Each person should attempt to use all three of his cards, but he can personally choose where and when to put them into the house.

   d. If at any point the house collapses, each person takes back his cards and then they begin again. Remember this should be done in silence; they must communicate in other ways than speaking.

   e. The first group to complete the task wins.

Set a time limit of about five minutes and announce the time remaining after each minute—e.g., four minutes left, three minutes left, etc.

V. STUDENT REACTION

When the time has expired or when one group wins, gather them for a discussion which should start with questions like the following:

1. How did it feel to have both the freedom to place the cards as you saw fit but also have the responsibility to place them in such a way as to not destroy the house and make the group start over?

2. Did you find yourself getting angry when others placed their cards in a way which you thought would not work, or in a way different than you would have done—or when they knocked down the house?

3. Was the inability to speak a real problem? Did anyone become a "leader" in your group and direct the operation? Would it have been helpful if someone had directed the effort?

4. Would it have worked better if everyone in your group had given their cards to the most adept and let him build the house alone? Would you like to try that as an experiment to see what it would feel like?

5. Can you see any relation to real life and this little exercise—say at school, in your family, with your friends, at work if you have a job?

INSTRUCTION ON FREEDOM

(Note to adult leader: *The outline below is intended as a sample outline on the topic. To be effective, it must be developed and adapted by you, that is, put into your own words and style, and filled out with sufficient examples taken from your own and the students' experience.*)

Introduction

As you have seen from our activity and discussion, it is one thing to say that every person has a right to be free within a group or society. It is not so easy to decide how to preserve the freedom of the individual and also that of the rest of the group or society.

Definition of Freedom

Forming some clear ideas of what we mean by freedom is the first step. Often the word "freedom" means different things to different people, so we must start the group by trying to decide what we all mean by freedom. As a way of beginning, I'll give a kind of definition and explain it. Then we can discuss it to see if you agree or disagree.

Most simply, freedom is "an ability to do those things which help a man become what he is supposed to become."

a. If you accept the idea of a core morality as we discussed it (cf. previous lesson), then we say a man is most free when he can do all those things which enable him to form friendships and cooperate with other persons.

b. So being free is not "doing what you want to do." It is being able to do what you are supposed to do. E.g., a man is not free if he hates someone, or if he is afraid of others, or if he can force others to obey him, or if he can't get along with others.

c. The secret of freedom, like that of deciding on core morality, is knowing what man is supposed to become. Since he is supposed to become someone who can live in a friendly relationship with others, whatever inside of him or outside of him prevents him from being able to do this is what makes him unfree.

d. More often than not, our lack of freedom comes from within us, not from outside us.

My definition of freedom, then, is this: the ability, both within and outside us, to do those things which enable us to live in friendship and cooperation with others.

Freedom Within a Group or Society

Since every man has a right to be free, what happens when one man disagrees with another on what will make for friendly relations?

Eg. One person in a group feels that the best thing he can do to promote friendship is rearrange the furniture we are sitting on, so people will be closer together. The rest of the group thinks the present arrangement is best for promoting friendship.

How do you resolve the conflict?

First principle: No two situations are exactly the same, so it is impossible to give an absolute answer for all cases. For example, we can't say that in every instance the group should yield to the individual; nor can we say that in every instance the individual should yield to the group.

Second principle: In any truly free society, the preservation of individual and group freedom depends on people's willingness to compromise, that is, adjust their original demands. This is not to say that compromises are always the solution (remember the first principle). It means we must at least be willing and able to compromise sometimes.

Third principle: Communication between the differing persons is essential. Often differences are more imagined than real. Often suitable compromises can be worked out for the best of all concerned. But we can't understand the real differences or come to any kind of mutual solution unless we continue to talk to the people with whom we disagree.

> E.g. In your family group, when you disagree with your parents, it does no good to turn them off. The only real way to become free—and allow them to be free—in that kind of situation is to keep in communication.

Fourth principle: Always be willing to reevaluate your own position. In other words, keep an open mind. You have enough experience to know that you have made some mistakes and that you will make some more. Are you sure your position will help you and others become what we are intended to be?

Fifth principle: Easy solutions, like dropping out or violence, seldom really solve the problem of insuring your and others' freedom. One side or the other usually loses freedom as a result. These principles obviously don't automatically solve the problem of individuals vs. group freedom. But they are involved in any solution you do work out. Briefly again they are:

    a. there are no pat answers
    b. compromise is often necessary
    c. communication is essential
    d. an open mind is always necessary
    e. "easy" solutions like force seldom work

Application and Summary

The essential elements in any successful group seem to be:

    1. mutual respect
    2. a common set of values or core morality
    3. individual and group freedom

We have defined freedom as your ability, both within yourself and in society, to do those things which best help you and others become what man is supposed to be.

The real problem comes when individuals and groups can't agree on what should be done.

This problem keeps coming up in all parts of life: family, school, church, government, marriage, business, etc. So it is naive to think we can escape it. What we need to do is learn how to work out the problem when it comes up, by using something like the five principles we mentioned.

FREEDOM

9

TH GRADE GROUPS

1 Do you think most ninth grade students have enough freedom? Do you think they really think about it that much? How do you think most ninth grade students would describe freedom? Would it be like we described it or would they consider it something else?

2 Do you think your classmates let you be free or does the group usually force the individuals to conform?

3 What do you think are some common things that all of us experience from inside us that keep us from being free? For example, fear of what others will say? Laziness, etc.?

4   Do you think there is too much or too little freedom given to ninth grade students by their parents? On the other hand, do you think most high school students ever think of the freedom that their parents deserve?

5   When an individual or a group of individuals can't agree with the majority on something, what do you think is the best way to handle it?

6   Would you say most ninth grade students are followers, or do you think they use their freedom to make up their own minds on what to do?

7   What are some things you would really like to do but you are not free to do? Would you end up hurting other people's freedom if you could do them? Would you end up doing some kind of harm to yourself if you had a chance to do them? What is keeping you back: lack of money, parents, education, laws, your own lack of effort, respect for other people's rights?

8   Do high school students know enough already to be allowed to help principals and teachers make school rules and decide on things like what should be taught, or is that something that only specialists should do?

9   How come little kids never worry about freedom, but older persons become very concerned?

10 Do you think most people really know what freedom is, or do you think they would define it as being able to get your own way?

FREEDOM

10

TH GRADE GROUPS

1 Do you think most tenth grade students have a good idea of what freedom is? How do you think most high school students would define freedom? Are they really concerned about freedom or is it just something to talk about and complain about?

2 Do you think your classmates let each person be free in the group or do you think that in most high schools the individual is pretty much forced to conform to the group's ideas—or be cut off from the group?

3 We often hear how parents don't give their children enough freedom. Do high schoolers talk much about the kind of freedom the parents deserve and if the kids allow parents to be free enough?

4   What do you think is the best solution when an
    individual's freedom and that of the larger group
    contradict each other? Have you ever been in that kind
    of bind as an individual? As a member of the group
    which is opposing the individual?

5   What kinds of things do you think most hold you back
    from becoming the kind of person you think you should
    be: other people, lack of money, lack of enough
    education or training, your respect for other people's
    rights, laws, your own inner lack of effort or discipline?
    Do you think others face the same kinds of problems with
    freedom as yourself?

6   Do tenth grade students know enough to be allowed to
    help principals and teachers make school rules, decide on
    classes to be taught, etc.? Do you agree with techniques
    like demands, student strikes, sit-ins, etc., to get student
    demands met? Do students have a right to make
    demands? What kind of demands do students not have
    the right to make? What happens when it is only a
    minority of students who want something?

7   Do you think most people are just followers and the only
    time they get upset is when someone tells them what they
    should do?

8   Who are the most unfree people in this city? Why? Can
    you explain what you mean by unfree? Is there anything
    you can or should do to help them become free?

9   When do you feel most unfree?

10 What could happen in this group which would make you
    feel unfree?

FREEDOM

TH GRADE GROUPS

1   Do you think most eleventh grade students would agree with the definition of freedom we used? If not, how do you think they would define it? How do you define it?

2   Is the complaint of lack of freedom within the home real for high school students or is it just something they like to complain about? Do most high school students allow their parents the same kind of freedom they expect to have?

3   Hippies talk a lot about freedom. What do you think they mean by freedom? Are they on the right track by dropping out in order to obtain their idea of freedom?

4   Something like the student demonstrations last year is a
    good example of two groups of people—administration
    and students—who could not agree on what was best for
    the school. Are demonstrations and things like sit-ins a
    good way to obtain freedom? Is calling the police a good
    way to preserve freedom? It is said that the vast majority
    of students weren't interested in the demands of the
    minority. Does the minority have the right to impose
    them on the majority? Does the majority have the right to
    use force to impose its ideas on the minority?

5   In your own school do you think most students know
    enough to help principals and teachers make school
    rules and decide on things like what should be taught? Do
    you think you have a right to make demands on the
    administration? What rights does the administration have
    in regard to its own freedom?

6   You've heard the statement "the truth will make you
    free." Do you think that it makes sense? How can truth
    make a person free?

7   What kinds of things most hold you back from being the
    kind of person you would like to be? Are these things
    imposed from outside you, or do they come from within
    yourself?

8   Do high school students allow each other to be free or
    does the majority pretty much decide what everyone will
    do—at the risk of being ignored and cut off from the
    group or being very unpopular?

9   Who are the most unfree people in our town? The most
    free people? Use your own definition of freedom to
    explain why you think so.

10 What one thing could your parents do that would really
    make you more free? What one thing could you do for
    your parents that would make them more free?

NECESSITY FOR DREAMING

The goal of the session is to help the students realize the role of having a dream or a goal in life and also to help them see how such a common dream or goal becomes one of the foundations for any society.

I. BEGINNING EXERCISE

The purpose of the exercise is to give the students an experience in dreaming, in reaching out, in imagining, in "shooting for the stars." (This is not such an impossible dream anymore.)

Instructions:

1. Divide your group into pairs or triads (groups of three).

2. Give each of these groups three everyday objects. Some examples of such objects are the following:

1. a straight pin, a rubber band, a burnt match
2. a magazine cover, a paper clip, a toothpick
3. a newspaper, a thumb tack, a piece of string
That should give you an idea of what is meant.

3. Now tell each group to plan together how they are going to use these items—their sole possessions—to begin a business or a project which will eventually make for them a million dollars.

N.B.: Stress that imagination should not be limited; encourage them to dream of ideal situations, of things that just work out. The only rule is that whatever they do must be both moral and logical. For example, they cannot use the pin to pick a lock on the bank safe, nor can they use the paper and toothpick to manufacture square circles which they sell.

They are not limited, however, to the earth. If they want to start an interplanetary business and sell bubble gum to Martians, that is fine, as long as they can explain how they can begin the business with what you gave them.

4. Give them about five to ten minutes to work out their plan. Then each group should explain it to the others. You may want to take a vote to decide which is the best or most feasible plan, but this is not necessary. It just adds incentive.

II. STUDENT REACTION

After each group has given its plan, you should seek their reactions by asking some of the following questions:

1. Did you think the whole thing was silly? Is it really possible for people to start with such small things and end up doing great things?

2. Would you have preferred to have been given some practical task like using the materials to build something?

3. Do any people really dream in this way? Is it a good way to live or is it foolish?

4. Did you find it hard to stay within the boundaries of accepted morality? of logic?

5. Did you find yourself kind of trapped by thinking of things like past failures or ideas like, "But this is just a fairy tale and things just don't happen the way we described them"? Were you too logical, in other words?

III. INSTRUCTION AND DISCUSSION

(The outline for the formal instruction and discussion questions are found at the end of the lesson.)

BREAK PERIOD

IV. SECOND EXERCISE

The purpose of this exercise is to apply the principle of dreaming to the students' own world. Although some concerted goal may emerge which they would like to pursue (in which case, encourage them) the success of the exercise does not depend on such a decision to actually go out and get something done.

Instructions:

1. Explain that you are going to ask them to do an exercise similar to the one they did earlier with three exceptions:

a. The whole group will do it together.
b. The materials they are to start with are:
    1. the talents of each person in the group, including adults
    2. one year of time
c. The goal is to change in some significant way their school; they must decide the precise goal, which may be anything from producing better school spirit to eliminating the use of dope.

2. The rules are the same; they must act morally and whatever they plan must be logical, even if it is "impossible" in terms of everyday experience—like getting the principal to come to one of their group meetings.

3. They must first decide on the goal and then decide on how they plan to achieve it, using the available talent and time.

4. Encourage them to dream, to reach, to be "impractical."

V. STUDENT REACTION

Once the group has decided on its goal and method of reaching it, you can begin discussion with some of the following questions:

1. Is what we talked about so out of reach—if we really knew how to dream and then to work for our dreams?

2. Do you feel uncomfortable with this kind of exercise—like it is too silly or too challenging?

3. Is there anything a group like this could not do if it really decided to do it and then went after it with discipline?

4. Would we need a leader to achieve our dream? Could we preserve each individual's freedom while pursuing the dream?

5. Would such a dream really help us direct change instead of letting change keep happening to us?

VI. ALTERNATE SECOND EXERCISE

Juniors and other older students might find "Rip Van Winkle" more stimulating.

Instructions:

Explain that the entire group has just fallen asleep. When we all wake we discover it is 20 years later, but we ourselves have not grown older.

Each person is to try to express what *hopes he would find* in his home town 20 years from now and also what he *probably would find*. After everyone who wishes has given his opinions, allow the students to ask questions of each other to explain more in detail why they said what they did. Then ask if their "hopes" are so impossible and what they could do to make them come true.

INSTRUCTION ON NECESSITY FOR DREAMING

(Note to adult leader: *The outline below is intended as a developed sample outline on the topic. To be effective, it must be developed and adapted by you, that is, put into your own words and style, and filled out with sufficient examples taken from your own and the students' experience.*)

Introduction

78 We have tried to get a feel for what it means to dream, to look out beyond the present into what could be, what we would like to see happen.

Now we want to see why it is important that every group, every society has a dream to shoot for.

Definition of a "dream" as we are using it:

A dream is another word for a goal. It is special in that it is a goal which we have no real assurance we will ever reach, but which we are willing to try to reach anyway. The goal is always to become what man is intended to be.

It may be a very personal and practical dream like the dream of becoming a doctor. It may be short range, like passing algebra. It may be long range like becoming the first man to land on Mars. It may be an "impossible dream" like starting a movement that will result in permanent world peace. It may be a dream you share with others, like the dream Negroes have for overcoming racial injustice.

A dream does not destroy the past; it often is rooted in it and builds on it. But a dream always directs for the future and always implies that we are willing in some degree to give up the past and foster change either in ourselves alone or in a whole group or country.

So a dream is a very special goal we set for ourselves, even though we have no guarantee that we will ever reach it. It is a goal we know we must work for, and we can't count on any immediate reward other than the satisfaction that we are working toward it.

Why Man Needs a Dream

1. Things in our lives keep changing; we keep changing physically, for example. The weather changes, the seasons change, we change schools, we move from one home to another, we change friends, clothes styles change, TV and movie heroes keep changing, music keeps changing. Our whole society, our whole world keeps changing around.

2. If you don't have a dream one of two things happens:

   a. You try to hang on to what you have—you try to resist change and keep things the way they are. This won't work and it leads to all kinds of new problems.

   E.g. Most mothers would like to keep their children babies and often, without realizing it, treat them as if they were babies. Sooner or later the children rebel and leave home, or at least they grow up and leave home. So a mother who resists the change in her children either harms the child or ends up very unhappy when the child does grow up.

   b. You let change keep happening to you. You give up your freedom to make things happen and let events and forces and other people shape you. You become a victim of circumstances, with no real control over your own future.

   E.g. Way back before the Second World War, the European people just let Hitler take over. They didn't agree with him but they did nothing to direct change. They let change, namely the change started by Hitler, change them.

E.g. Some people keep building on a riverbank even though it overflows each year. They don't move their house or build a dam. They just move when the river forces them out.

3. If you have a dream several things happen:

   a. You don't resist change as such. In fact, you encourage it, you accept it as an important part of your human situation.

   b. Because of your dream, you learn to control the forces of change—you cooperate with good changes and you resist those that tend to destroy your dream.

   c. Because it is a dream, you know it can't be realized at once, that you must work toward it, that you must put up with the present without surrendering to it. A dream gives your life purpose; and if your life has purpose, you can direct your talents and energies toward that purpose. Life becomes exciting and meaningful *now* because you have a dream for tomorrow.

   d. So a dream becomes a vital, unifying force. It equips you to live within a world of constant change, yet gives direction and meaning.

4. Groups and society need dreams too:

   a. Groups and society, like the USA, are just like individuals. They need to have a common dream to survive.

   b. When a group doesn't have a dream it tends to try to resist change, hang on to the past, turn in on itself. It spends all its energy thinking about what it had and trying to preserve what it has. A group without a dream is an enemy of progress.

c. A group with a dream goes outside itself, remains open to change and growth, allows new ideas and new people to influence it so it can reach its dream.

d. So a dream unifies a group in much the same way as a core morality does. The dream and the morality are usually two sides of the same thing. A dream gives a group a goal, a sense of direction and meaning and purpose. If a group doesn't have these things it soon dies.

Summary

1. We have defined a dream as a goal we have no assurance of reaching, but which we strive for nonetheless, because it is both possible and worth giving ourselves to.

2. Dreams help us live creatively in a world of constant change.

3. Dreams keep us from turning in on ourselves and turning to the past; they keep us open to new experiences, new people, the future.

4. Dreams give our life meaning and purpose; they help us direct and use our talents and our present situation in positive, productive ways.

NECESSITY FOR DREAMING

9 TH GRADE GROUPS

1 Do you agree that people need to have a dream? Do you think most ninth-grade students have a dream or goal? What kind of dreams would you think are typical of a junior high student?

2 Do dreams really help people live with change? Does change really worry ninth-grade students that much? Do they look forward to change, fear it, let it happen to them or do they direct change with their dreams?

3 Have you ever shared a dream with someone? Does it really bind you close together?

4   Do you think most ninth-grade students are capable of long-range or "impossible" dreams or do they need more immediate and short-range practical dreams?

5   Do you think most adults have dreams? Do parents have dreams? Do dreams really shape people's lives that much? Or do they just fill in spare time with no practical value?

6   Does America have any kind of dream? What do you think it is? Do you share it? Why or why not?

7   What kind of dreams do you think a group like this could share? What do you think would happen to this group if we all began to share a common dream?

8   High school and college students are often called dreamers. From your experience is this accurate? Is it good? Why do young people seem to dream more than older people? Or do they really?

9   Do you have a dream? Would you share it with the group, assuming that no one would laugh at anyone else's dream? Have you ever really been encouraged to dream before? By whom? Does your school encourage you to dream?

10 What happens to people who don't have a dream? Are they practical, or do they become victims of change? What kind of dreams do you think poor people have? Negroes?

NECESSITY FOR DREAMING

TH GRADE GROUPS

1 Do you think most tenth grade groups would agree that dreaming is important? What kind of dreams would be typical of this age group?

2 How do most sophomores regard change? Is it something to enjoy? to endure? to resist or to use and direct? Why do young people seem to enjoy change and older people seem to resist it?

3   Would you say that your school encourages or discourages you from developing your own dream? Why? Should there be a course in dreaming?

4   Have you ever known a group who shared a dream? Can you describe how they acted? Did their dream really bind them together and help them shape their future or was it just a dream—all talk?

5   Can you think of any great dreamers in history? Did their dreaming really shape themselves and others? What are some of the qualities of a really good dreamer?

6   What do you think would happen to this group if we shared a common dream? Can you think of any kinds of dreams we could share in common?

7   Is it true that most dreamers tend to be less selfish and more outer directed or concerned with others than people who don't dream? Can you think of examples of this?

8   Is it hard to be a dreamer in our society, with all the pressures and all the demands to perform immediate, practical tasks?

9   Do you think having a dream, a real dream, would make you more disciplined than if you did not have one?

10   Does America have a common dream? What do you think it is? Or what do you think it *should* be? Could you get excited and share America's dream?

NECESSITY FOR DREAMING

11

TH GRADE GROUPS

1   Is the world really changing as much as we said? Is
change such a problem for high school students? What
kinds of change bother them the most? How do most high
school students handle change? Let it happen to them?
Resist it? Promote it? Use and direct it?

2   Is dreaming really practical or will the man with a dream
be run over by the system which is too busy making a
living *now?*

3 What kinds of dreams or goals do you think most high school juniors have? Do they share these in common or are they private and personal dreams? Does your school (student body) have a dream which guides and directs them as a group?

4 What would happen to this group if it developed a common dream? What kind of common dream should (or could) a group like this have? Can a group like this survive without a common dream?

5 You usually hear that high school and college students are dreamers and idealists. From your acquaintance with this age group, would you say that this is true? Why? Do you think it is good or bad?

6 Do you think your school encourages dreaming in the way we have described it? Should schools offer a course in dreaming? Are all courses potentially courses in dreaming?

7 Does our society have a dream? If it does, how would you describe it? Could you share such a dream?

8 Can you think of any great things that have happened in our country because an individual or a group had a dream? Is dreaming really all that easy or is it hard work which takes a lot of discipline once you pursue your dream?

9 Do you think most adults have a dream, for example, our parents? What kinds of dreams do they have? Are they much different from dreams of young people? Why? Is this good or bad?

10 Do you have a dream? Would you share it with us, assuming no one would laugh at another person's dream, no matter how "impossible" it may sound?

THE GOSPEL DREAM

This session is intended to relate the Gospel to all that has taken place in previous meetings. It is not intended to give a detailed description of all the truths in the Gospel. Instead it is intended to help students see where the Gospel fits into their own lives.

I. BEGINNING EXERCISE

The purpose of the exercise is to "beg the question" in one sense. By presenting the Gospel together with other "books" as containing a dream, we want to initiate the students into the attitude of regarding the Gospel as a dream, a challenge, a goal, and free them from regarding it as some out-of-touch set of rules.

Note:

It is suggested that you provide some old magazines, paste, scissors, etc., so the students can make collages. Since this takes some time, you will not need a second exercise in this session. Therefore, take your break after everyone has finished his collage. When you reassemble, have the groups explain their work, move into the lesson and then end with questions and general discussion.

Instructions:

1. Place on the table or on the floor in the middle of the group three "books."
   a. A New Testament.
   b. A popular magazine like *Time, Life, Sports Illustrated* or a representative combination of such magazines.
   c. Any book or magazine representative of science—e.g., a chemistry textbook, science fiction novel, etc., or a combination of such books.

2. Divide the students into three small groups. Provide each group with a sheet of poster paper. Have some marking pens or crayons available.

3. Explain that each "book" attempts to say something about man and man's dreams. Each book in its own way attempts to give man a dream.

   Group A should attempt to symbolize on its poster what the Gospel says about man and the kind of dream it attempts to give man.

   Group B should do the same for the popular magazines —stressing that it should be as positive as possible.

   Group C should do the same for the science books.

BREAK PERIOD

II. STUDENT REACTION

When you reassemble, ask the students to compare their posters, looking for the following things in them:

1. Any similarity in the idea of what man is and what the dream is.

2. Any contrasts or contradictions.

3. Which one really says the most to them, which one seems most unrealistic about life—as they experience life themselves?

4. Which dream seems most realistic, which one most unrealistic—do the books really present a dream for man at all, etc?

5. Did we leave out any important "book" that should be represented?

From this you want to move into a discussion of the role of the Gospel in the life of modern man, especially the high school student, and then go into discussion on the nature of the Gospel as a dream for man.

III. INSTRUCTION AND DISCUSSION

(The outline for the formal instruction and discussion questions can be found at the end of this lesson.)

IV. SECOND EXERCISE

Since the dream the Gospel presents is eternal life and eternal friendship, it can't really be appreciated until men are more aware of what death and isolation would be like. This exercise is intended to give the students an imaginative experience of "death." Since it is rather sophisticated, it will be effective only with more mature students.

Instructions:

1. Have everyone stand in a tight circle in the center of the room, their arms interlocked. Tell them to either sing or talk together until you give them a signal to stop. You should have a record or some form of music (radio, tape, etc.) on in the background—and if possible on high volume.

2. When you feel they are all talking or laughing or singing —that is, somehow quite involved with each other—tell them to stop and remain silent. After a few seconds, turn off the music, by slowing down the volume until it goes off.

3. Now ask them to disengage their arms and turn around, but remain in the circle.

4. Next, ask them to take several steps outward, away from each other, then a few more until finally they are as far apart as they can get in the room.

5. Finally, ask each person to sit down wherever he is, close his eyes and draw himself into as tight a ball as he can get into.

   ALL OF THIS IS DONE IN SILENCE SO ASK THEM TO COOPERATE.

6. If possible, at this point, turn out all the lights in the room, advising them ahead of time that the lights will be out for three minutes and during that time they should remain silent, eyes closed, in a tight ball (please, no giggling, etc.). After about *one minute*—if it is quiet—turn on the lights and ask them to reassemble for discussion.

V. STUDENT REACTION

Begin by asking how long they felt the lights were out. Ask about their impressions, what they experienced, felt and thought about as they gradually withdrew from each other.

Then ask them if they see any similarity between this and what it would mean to die. From this go into a discussion about what death means to them and finally if the promise of the Gospel can make sense only after people are more aware of what it would mean to die and be isolated from everyone.

This can be a very effective exercise provided the students can do it seriously and you can achieve the desired effect of gradual withdrawal, silence and isolation.

OUTLINE

INSTRUCTION ON THE GOSPEL DREAM

(Note to adult leader: *The outline below is intended as a sample outline on the topic. To be effective, it must be developed and adapted by you, that is, put into your own words and style, and filled out with sufficient examples taken from your own and the students' experience.*)

Introduction

In the last session we saw that it is very important for every person and group to have a dream. It is part of being human; it is what helps us understand the necessary element of change in human life; it is what turns us out of ourselves and directs us toward others and toward the future; it is what gives our lives meaning, purpose and direction.

It is the conviction of Christians that the Gospel presents man with a very special dream; the dream God has for man. So we want to take a quick look at what the Gospel says—you know it pretty well already—but this time look at it in terms of being a dream or goal for all men, a dream that will make us really human.

The Dream in the Gospel

1. The main dream or goal that Jesus presents—and it certainly is a dream—is that all men learn to be friends with one another and consequently with God, the Father of all men.

   This is not a far-out or "inhuman" dream in terms of the core morality we spoke about earlier. Man seems intended to learn how to be friends with other men. So the main dream of the Gospel is that men learn how to be truly human. In the face of all the hatred, war, injustice and cruelty that we see in history and in our own day, that is quite a dream, one that would take a lot of work to achieve.

Too often we think the Gospel presents some "pie in the sky dream" of heaven after we die. The real dream of the Gospel is for men to become truly human on earth. For this reason, the Gospel is intended to be a common dream, one a whole group or community of people strives for. It's not some personal thing only, like saving my soul. To save your soul really means to learn how to become friends with others—which means you are automatically involved with the other guy.

2. The Gospel's dream has one other important dimension. It dreams of a mankind that lives in friendship *forever*. So it dreams of an eternal, not just a temporary life. It dreams of a mankind that conquers death, since death more than anything else separates us from one another. This was the "impossible dream" that turned on the early Christians once they became convinced that Jesus had conquered death and promised them the same chance.

Is the Gospel Dream Unique?

1. Jesus and his followers weren't the first or the last to dream of a united mankind. Other religious leaders and groups have had similar dreams.

2. What makes the Gospel dream different is the conviction Christians have that Jesus is God, that he still lives among us, that he is helping mankind reach this dream, and most importantly, that he promises a permanent fulfillment of the dream—a community of men who will live forever.

   No other person ever dared to have that kind of dream— and the reason is no other person ever conquered death itself.

3. So what makes a Christian different from other men is his having a bigger dream than other men. A true Christian (to be distinguished from all those who call themselves Christian but don't share Jesus' dream) is not less human than other men; he is more human; he dreams about a mankind that becomes perfectly human.

Does a Christian Act Differently From Other Good Men?

1. No, if you mean by different that a Christian would be less concerned about the problems man faces today: disease, hunger, racial injustice, poverty, war, loneliness, hatred. Nor is the Christian less concerned about the goals that man is engaged in: conquest of the material universe through science, better education, housing, medical care, government, etc.

2. The Christian's dream is a very human dream which immerses him very much in human life. His dream is to become perfectly human, which means to learn how to live as friends with other men.

3. The Christian is different in only one way—but it is a big one. He accepts Jesus as his God and he believes that Jesus shares very much in his own efforts to become human. This conviction gives the true Christian a courage and optimism and spirit of joy which enables him to work harder at his dream than most men can.

Summary

1. The Gospel does present a dream to men, the dream that Jesus had.

2. This dream is the goal of a perfect human friendship among all men forever.

3. The dream is intended to be held in common by a group or community, since it is not a private or personal dream, like dreaming of becoming a doctor or professional basketball player.

4. It is unique because it is God's dream shared by men and it shoots for a totally perfect mankind that will live forever.

5. A Christian is unique only in that he is convinced that the Gospel is God's dream for man and that Jesus is God. He is not unique in what he does, but only in why he does it.

THE GOSPEL DREAM

9

TH GRADE GROUPS

1 Is the Gospel the kind of dream most ninth grade students can get excited about? Why or why not? Has it ever been presented to you as a dream? Do you think it could be a dream worth getting excited about?

2 What would happen at your school or in your class if all the kids suddenly got excited about the Gospel dream and made it their goal? What practical changes would begin to take place? In what ways does your school seem to act contrary to the Gospel dream?

3 Is the Gospel really that much different from the kind of thing advocated by the UN or by the government? What makes it different in your eyes, if you think it is different?

4 Why are most kids turned off when you start talking about the Gospel? Why don't kids like to be labeled "good" or "religious" or "holy"? Is religion, real religion, like what the Gospel tries to get across, phony? Or does it make sense?

5 Can men ever really be friends with one another? What holds us back the most? What holds *you* back from liking and being friends with everyone?

6 If religion is not intended as a gimmick or an insurance policy which guarantees that you "save your soul," then what is religion? What did Jesus really try to say and to show by his life and his death and resurrection?

7 We said that the Christian is different from other men in only one thing, though it is a big one: He believes that Jesus is God and so he believes that he shares in the dream God has for men. Are most ninth grade students really interested in God? Are they even old enough to ask intelligent questions about God? Is the question of God something you talk about much in your everyday conversations? Would you usually be laughed at if you tried? Why?

8 If a Christian is someone who has the Gospel for his dream, do you think you are a Christian?

9 Is Christianity or the Gospel really as complicated and as hard to understand as it has been made out to be? How would you personally summarize the main ideas of Christianity and the Gospel? Are they that much different from your instinct about what is right and wrong?

10 Do you think the Gospel dream is intended for a community of people or can each man handle it and make it work on its own? In other words, is a Church really necessary if the Gospel dream is to be realized?

THE GOSPEL DREAM

10

TH GRADE GROUPS

98

1 Is the Gospel the kind of dream most tenth grade students can get excited about? Why or why not? Has it ever been presented to you as a dream? Do you think it could be a dream worth getting excited about?

2 What would happen at your school or in your class if all the kids suddenly got excited about the Gospel dream and made it their goal? What practical changes would begin to take place? In what ways does your school seem to act contrary to the Gospel dream?

3 Is the Gospel really that much different from the kind of thing advocated by the UN or by the government? What makes it different in your eyes, if you think it is different?

4 Why are most kids turned off when you start talking about the Gospel? Why don't kids like to be labeled "good" or "religious" or "holy"? Is religion, like what the Gospel tries to get across, phony? Or does it make sense?

5 Can men ever really be friends with one another? What holds us back the most? What holds *you* back from liking and being friends with everyone?

6 If religion is not intended as a gimmick or an insurance policy which guarantees that you "save your soul," then what is religion? What did Jesus really try to say and to show by his life and his death and resurrection?

7 We said that the Christian is different from other men in only one thing, though it is a big one: He believes that Jesus is God and so he believes that he shares in the dream God has for men. Are most tenth grade students really interested in God? Are they even old enough to ask intelligent questions about God? Is the question of God something you talk about much in your everyday conversations? Would you usually be laughed at if you tried? Why?

8 If a Christian is someone who has the Gospel for his dream, do you think you are a Christian?

9 Is Christianity or the Gospel really as complicated and as hard to understand as it has been made out to be? How would you personally summarize the main ideas of Christianity and the Gospel? Are they that much different from your instinct about what is right and wrong?

10 Do you think the Gospel dream is intended for a community of people or can each man handle it and make it work for himself? In other words, is a Church really necessary if the Gospel dream is to be realized?

THE GOSPEL DREAM

TH GRADE GROUPS

1 Is the Gospel the kind of dream most eleventh grade students could get excited about? Do you think most high school students really understand the full idea behind the dream of Jesus: friendship with all men *forever?*

2 If we dreamed a little and supposed your whole high school suddenly became excited about the Gospel and made it their common dream, what kinds of *practical* changes do you think you would see in the way the students acted, and what they tried to accomplish? Would they become less human in the process? Would they become "pious" and "holy," or would they still be interested in just "having fun"?

3 If Christianity is more a challenge than an insurance policy which guarantees that you will "save your soul" if you play by the rules, why hasn't it been taught that way? What is religion really all about if it is not a discipline for saving your soul?

4 How would you summarize the main ideas of the Gospel and Christianity?

5 Why are most kids turned off by religion? Why do they fear being labeled "holy" or "good" or "religious"? Why are so few interested in learning more about the Gospel if it really is a dream which is intended to make all men friends?

6 Does the Gospel dream really have to be shared by a community or group of people in order to work? Can it be just a personal dream each man works out in his own way? In other words, do we really need a Church in order to make the Gospel dream work?

7 Do you think all men can ever learn to live in friendship and peace or is this just an "impossible" dream? What is the goal of men if it is not the goal presented by Jesus in the Gospel?

8 Why are girls more often turned on by religion than boys? Is religion for weak people or for those who have the most guts?

9 Does the Gospel really try to develop a perfectly human society or does it distort human nature and make unreal demands on it which makes us into half-human people?

THE CHURCH

The goal of this session is twofold. It should allow the students to express their own frustration or objections to the Church, thus providing an outlet for negative feelings. Second, it should give them some basic understanding and appreciation of the Church objectively.

Note: Do not become defensive if the students are critical of the Church. Allow them to express these feelings before you present the positive side.

I. BEGINNING EXERCISE

The purpose of the exercise is to give the students a tangible experience of various human relationships and society structures. This exercise can also tell them a great deal about themselves and how they relate to others. It is important that you are observant during this exercise and during the reaction session.

Instructions:

1. Ask each student to simply walk (mill) about the room in any direction and to stop at whatever place and in whatever position he feels most comfortable. This should be done in silence.

2. When everyone has stopped moving, ask them to observe and remember just where they ended up and look around to notice where others ended up.

3. Then ask them to form a circle by joining hands. Then ask them to get closer and interlock their arms. Then ask them to disengage, then to remain in the circle and turn around, facing outward, but hold hands again, and finally still facing outward, ask them to join arms again **103** so they are very close but together facing outward.

   N.B.: PAUSE BRIEFLY BETWEEN EACH CHANGE OF POSITION SO THEY GET USED TO BEING IN THE NEW POSITION—STRESS THAT THIS SHOULD ALL BE DONE IN SILENCE.

4. Ask them to form one line and close their eyes, put their hands on the shoulders of the person in front of them. You get in front of the line, with eyes open, and tell them to follow you with their eyes still closed. Move about enough so that each person has had to take at least several steps.

II. STUDENT REACTION

Finally ask them to sit down for the beginning of the discussion, which should be started by some of the following questions:

1. Which formation did you feel most comfortable in— why?

2. Which formation seems to best symbolize how your high school relates to you as an individual?

3. Which formation or position best symbolized how you see yourself in relation to the rest of society?

4. Which formation did you like the most in terms of relating to others?

5. Which formation best symbolized how the Church is organized—why?

From this point on explore their feelings about the Church, but be willing to remain on other points, such as their feelings toward their high school or themselves in society.

This can be a very self-revealing exercise but quite non-threatening.

III. INSTRUCTION AND DISCUSSION

(The outline for the formal instruction and discussion questions are found at the end of this lesson.)

BREAK PERIOD

IV. SECOND EXERCISE

This exercise is designed to give the students a tangible experience of Church structure and where they fit into it—or where they think they should.

Instructions:

1. Prepare ahead of time two sets of paper cups on which you have written the following:

    a. one cup with "bishop" and one with "priest"
    b. several cups with "adult laity"
    c. several cups with "youth"
    d. several cups with "small children"

2. Divide the students into two groups and give each group a set of cups. Ask Group A to arrange their cups into the formation they think best represents how the Church is actually structured. (They can do this on a table or on the floor.) Group B should arrange its cups into a formation that they think best represents how the Church and the people in it should be related to each other.

3. After each group has done its project, have a volunteer from each group explain the group's formation. Others are then free to challenge the formations and give reasons why the formations should be rearranged. If they can convince the rest, have them rearrange the formations until everyone is satisfied.

V. STUDENT REACTION

Afterwards, ask them to explain why they feel that way, what they can do to bring about the change in Church structure, etc. From this move into your general discussion on the nature of the Church (see discussion questions).

VI. ALTERNATE SECOND EXERCISE

Instructions:

1. Divide the students into two smaller groups and then take one person from each of the groups—or ask for a volunteer.

2. The two volunteers are to assume the role of clergy-hierarchy. Group A is to assume the role of adult Church members. Group B is to assume the role of high school age Church members.

3. The clergy and the two groups are then to form some kind of formation which symbolizes how they think the Church is actually structured today—e.g., maybe the younger group would all go over in a corner and turn their backs on the rest and all the adults would stand in one line behind the priests and the priests get on chairs.

4. After they have done that, ask them to stay in the same groups but now form some formation which would symbolize how the Church should be structured as far as they are concerned.

INSTRUCTION ON THE CHURCH

(Note to adult leader: *The outline below is intended as a sample outline of the topic. To be effective, it must be developed and adapted by you, that is, put into your own words and style, and filled out with sufficient examples taken from your own and the students' experience.*)

Introduction

In our meetings so far we have seen that an ideal group or society has certain qualities:

— mutual respect among the members
— a core morality or set of values
— individual and group freedom
— a dream or goal

We defined the Church as a group of people or a society which is founded on mutual respect, possesses a core morality, protects personal freedom and has a dream. What makes the Church different from other groups or communities is its dream which is the dream of Jesus, namely, the Gospel.

We want to briefly test out this definition or rather, show how we can. We will examine the Church in these four areas to see if it measures up.

Officially because of your baptism and your family background you belong to this Church or society. In fact, no one belongs until he shares the dream of Jesus and makes it his own, which implies he also accepts the core morality of the Church and cooperates with other Christians in striving for this dream.

So what we are really trying to do is help you see reasons why you should or should not belong to the Church as you become adults.

We aren't saying the Church is perfect. But we are saying that it has the best potential for helping man realize his real goal of friendship and everlasting life with all men.

So to belong to the Church is also to accept the task of putting up with its imperfections and working to improve them, while you also strive to realize the dream of the Gospel.

Church and Mutual Respect

1. The early Church certainly was known for the amount of concern or respect the members showed others. Brotherly love, mutual help, active concern were all very obvious when Christians came together.

2. This same ideal has certainly been preached since that time on, but it would be naive to say the Church has always succeeded in showing mutual respect among members.

3. Today, I think it would be safe to say that the Church still considers mutual respect and brotherly love essential, but it doesn't always practice it equally. So we will want to see in what ways the Church does continue to show this respect for all men, and areas in which the Church seems to be failing.

The Church and a Core Morality

1. The core morality of the Church seems to be summed up in the two great commandments of Jesus: love of God and neighbor.

2. This morality, like any morality, is based on a particular understanding of man's nature. The Church, following the teaching of Jesus, thinks that man is destined to live forever in friendship with all his fellowmen.

3. The "laws" of the Church regarding right and wrong are all based on this view of man.

4. So while there may be some disagreement in applying these "laws" to specific situations (e.g., birth control) it seems safe to say that the Church does have a core morality.

Freedom and the Church

1. The Church certainly maintains the absolute importance of freedom for the individual. It is very much in keeping with Jesus' teaching about the nature of man.

2. However, the Church is having quite a time today with the dilemma we talked about regarding freedom: how to protect the freedom of individuals and also maintain the freedom of the group.

   This seems to be a key problem in the Church today, but we shouldn't be surprised if we recall what we said about freedom and how hard it is at times to work out individual and group freedom.

3. So the Church can be an ideal community and still have problems about freedom. All truly free groups do. Our concern is with how the Church is working out these problems. We will want your comments about the problems and possible solutions.

The Church's Dream

1. The Gospel vision of man and what man can become is the Church's dream. It has spent the last 2,000 years roaming all over the world proclaiming that dream and trying to make it work by founding hospitals, schools, orphanages, fighting for social justice, etc.

2. Today, however, there is much criticism that the Church no longer has a dream. It is simply trying to preserve itself and so it resists change and has turned in on itself.

3. Like any criticism, this is partially true and partially false. It should be our task to try to see to what extent it has lost it.

THE CHURCH

9TH GRADE GROUPS

1 Do you think the Church has much mutual respect within it? Have you in general been treated with respect within the Church? When do you feel you haven't received this respect from other Catholics?

2 Does the Church as a community or group have much to offer most ninth grade students, that is, what are some reasons ninth grade students would want to be members of the Church? What are some reasons why they would not want to be members of the Church?

3 Have you ever thought of the Church as an ideal community? How would you describe the Church, based on your experience of it so far?

4 How would you describe the Church's core morality? Is it the kind of core morality that makes sense to most ninth grade students? Does it really seem that much different from the core morality we talked about in an earlier session?

5 Does it surprise you that there is a disagreement over how this core morality should be applied, for example in things like birth control? Can you think of any aspect of the Church's teaching on morality that most ninth grade students don't agree with? Are you sure you are talking about morality?

6 Is there freedom in the Church as far as most ninth grade students are concerned? How does the Church seem to work out the problem of individual vs. group freedom? Can you think of any major problem of this kind in the Church today? What do you think is the best solution to it (e.g., priestly celibacy)?

7 Does the Church seem to have a common dream today? What is it in your opinion? Or has the Church lost its earlier dream? Why do you think so? Is the Church too turned in on itself, too concerned about protecting itself, not concerned enough about the present and future?

8 Why do you really belong to the Church? Do you think you will still belong when you become an adult?

9 Is there anything a ninth grade student can do *now* to help the Church become an ideal community? If the Church were an ideal community in our town, what kind of effect do you think it would have?

10 Do you think Jesus is pleased with the way his Church has turned out? If not, what kind of changes do you think he would make today within his Church?

THE CHURCH

Q U E S T I O N S

10

TH GRADE GROUPS

1 Do you think the Church has much to offer the average tenth grade student? What are some typical reasons why high school students belong to the Church? Why are some dropping out?

2 Can you think of times when you received respect from other members of the Church? Can you think of situations where you did not get this respect? Why?

3 How would you describe the Church to someone? As an ideal community? In what ways is it not an ideal community? Based on your own experience of the Church, does it have the key elements needed for any successful community or group?

4 How would you describe the Church's core morality? Is it the kind of core morality that makes sense to most high school students? If not, what are some things that don't make sense? Why do you think there is so much disagreement today over how the core morality should be practiced, e.g., birth control?

5 As a member of the Church, do you think you are free? Does the Church protect the freedom of individuals within it? How does it work out the problem of individual vs. group freedom? What seems to be the biggest problem of this kind in the Church today? Can you suggest a solution?

6 Does the Church still have the dream it had when it started? In what ways do you think it has lost the dream, if you feel it has? Without its dream, does the Church have much to offer the world? **113**

7 Why do you really belong to the Church? Do you think you will belong when you are an adult? Would you encourage others to join?

8 Is there anything a tenth grade student can do *now* to help the Church become the ideal community? Why does the Church bother to have discussion groups like this for you? What do you think is the goal of them?

9 Do you think Jesus is pleased with his Church today? If not, what kind of changes do you think he would make within his Church today?

10 If the Church were an ideal community in our town, what kind of effects would it have on the populace? What kind of effects is the Church having on our town?

THE CHURCH

11

TH GRADE GROUPS

1 Is it true that most high school students are turned off by the Church? If this is true, why do you think it is so? Is there anything they have found that is a good substitute for what the Church stands for and is trying to achieve?

2 We described the Church as a community or group that is potentially ideal. How would you describe the Church? What has been your experience of the Church? Have you been treated with respect within the Church? Have you experienced it as a community with a common dream, a common morality and with freedom for its members?

3   Insofar as there is disagreement between the general idea of core morality within the Church and how this is to be done in practice (e.g., birth control) how are such differences to be worked out?

4   How would you describe the core morality of the Church? Does it say anything to high school students? Is it much different from what we described as core morality in an earlier session?

5   How would you describe the dream of the Church? Is the dream being pursued today? If not, why do you think the Church is not pursuing its dream? What would happen in our town if all the Catholic churches pursued this dream seriously?

6   Does the Church give freedom to the high school student? In what areas don't you feel free as a member of the Church? How does the Church work out the problem of individual vs. group freedom? Can the Church or any group survive if there is no central authority?

7   Why are you a Catholic today? Would you encourage friends to join the Church? Do you think you will remain in the Church as an adult? What alternatives are open to you if you believe that Jesus is God? What about your children? Will you want them to be Catholics?

8   Assuming the Church has some faults right now, is there anything that high school students can do *now* to help the Church overcome them and come closer to its ideal?

9   What kind of changes do you think Jesus wants for his Church today?

10 Do young people like yourselves need a community like the Church or can you find what you need in other places and organizations? Why do you think the Church sponsors discussion groups like this one?

THE CHURCH'S MISSION

The purpose of the session is to help students experience the nature of the Church's mission and to free them from misconceptions about that mission. Finally, the goal is to help them discover their role in that mission.

I. BEGINNING EXERCISE

The purpose of this exercise is to give the students an experience of the prophetic nature of the Church's mission and how the Church should try to guide others without using force or power—and how some hinder her work with false advice.

Instructions:

    1. Ask for four to six volunteers. Form them into two-person teams.

2. Line up one member from each team in the middle of the room. About six inches to a foot directly in front of them place a paper cup.

   Line up each teammate opposite his partner about six feet away. Give each one a penny or similar object. Blindfold them or at least ask them to keep their eyes tightly shut. They are to put one hand behind their back.

3. When the teams are ready, explain the object and the rules:

a. The man with the cup at his feet is to try to direct his partner in such a way that he can find the cup and place the penny in it. He can help only by *instructions*. He *cannot touch* the cup, his partner or the coin.

b. Those not participating directly should try either to help or confuse the contestants by giving their own (false) instructions.

c. The first team to get its coin in the cup wins.

II. STUDENT REACTION

After one team wins, reassemble the group and seek their reactions to the exercise by some of the following questions:

1. To those blindfolded: Did you find it difficult to hear your partner's instructions and recognize his voice? When you heard them, could you understand what he was asking you to do? Did you find the whole thing kind of awkward and frustrating? Do you think with practice with your partner you could get pretty good at that kind of exercise?

2. To those who had to give the instructions: Did you find it hard getting your instructions across? Did you find it frustrating not being able to touch or guide your partner in some physical way?

3. To everyone: Can you think of any real life situations which are similar to this game? For example, times when you are really "blind" or confused and looking for advice and you hear all kinds of conflicting advice.

Once you get them to discuss life situations which are somewhat similar—they are looking for direction but hear all kinds of conflicting advice—then move into the formal instruction on the mission of the Church.

III. INSTRUCTION AND DISCUSSION

(The outline for the formal instruction and discussion questions are found at the end of this lesson.)

BREAK PERIOD

IV. SECOND EXERCISE

The purpose of this exercise is to give the students an experience of how the Church must work in concrete situations like those of unjust distribution of wealth.

Instructions:

1. Ask for three volunteers. Divide the rest of the students into two groups.

2. Give everyone in Group A an empty paper cup, ask them to sit down somewhere on the floor and remain silent. Give each person in Group B a paper cup with two pennies in it.

3. Explain that those with empty cups represent the poor. Because they are poor they can neither move about nor do anything to help themselves. Those with the pennies represent the wealthy. Because they have money they can move about and talk.

4. The three volunteers represent the "Church" and their mission is to attempt to get the wealthy to share with the poor. They must decide on a way to do this, but they cannot use force or trickery.

Finally, explain that the wealthy should not share their money until the "Church" has convinced them why they should.

Give about five-ten minutes for the "Church" to accomplish its mission. Call time if they don't succeed.

V. STUDENT REACTION

After the exercise, begin the student reaction and discussion about the Church's mission with some of the following questions:

1. How did it feel to be "poor," unable to help yourselves, forced to remain silent and unable to move about? To watch others try to help and fail?

2. If anyone did give up his penny to the "poor," ask him what really convinced him he should.

Those—it may be all the wealthy—who did not give up their pennies should be asked why they weren't convinced and what the Church would have had to do to convince them.

3. The "wealthy" should be asked if they appreciated their power to move and speak, that is, their independence in relation to the poor.

4. The "Church" should be asked how they felt when they succeeded and when they failed to succeed. Did they feel frustrated, tempted to use force or trickery or threats to get the others to share?

From this you can go into a general discussion of the Church and how it should go about its mission.

INSTRUCTION ON THE CHURCH'S MISSION

(Note to adult leader: *The outline below is intended as a sample outline for the topic. To be effective it must be developed and adapted by you, that is, put into your own words and style and filled out with suggestions and examples from your own and the students' experience.*)

Introduction

We saw in the previous meeting that the Church is at least potentially an ideal community with the dream or goal of helping all men become friends and fulfill their human nature. **121**

Now we want to explore just how the Church is attempting to do this—or is failing to do it.

How the Church Works in Society

1. To start out we want to point out a few common mistakes regarding the Church which confuse people, even members of the Church:

a. The Church is not intended to be a political or economic force in society. That is, it is not intended to use these common means to influence people to live the Gospel.

b. The Church is not intended to build and own charitable institutions (hospitals, etc.) except in those cases where society refuses to perform these needed services. This doesn't mean it can't run these kinds of programs, but there is nothing about the Church which says it must.

It is important to realize this because too often the Church is criticized for not doing enough in society by way of politics, for example. On the other hand, too often Christians have felt that unless they are running some big charitable work like an orphanage, they are not being Christian.

2. The Church actually works in society to promote the dream of the Gospel in only one way—by teaching the Gospel to its members and others. It teaches in two ways:

a. In programs like this it attempts to help people like yourselves understand what the Gospel and Jesus are really all about.

b. By the example of Christians like yourselves who go out into society—be it politics, social work, or just plain living and earning a living—and apply the Gospel to your own situation.

So the Church is not a "power structure." It's a group of little people who share a dream and who live out that dream in their daily lives. The Church needs organizations for only one thing: to teach its members and help them celebrate together.

So it is unfair to criticize the Church for not being a direct political force, for example, by backing some candidate, or for not setting up organizations to eliminate poverty or racial injustice.

The Church has one mission, to announce the Gospel. Those who hear it and who are already in society then have the obligation to use the means society provides to bring men to true brotherhood. So the real work of the Church is to keep alive the dream of Jesus, and to challenge those who are opposing that dream and degrading man in the process.

The Church and Social Issues

Let's list a few social issues which may be affecting you or will affect you shortly:

a. the drug problem among youth
b. the generation gap
c. shop lifting, stealing at school, vandalism
d. the sex revolution
e. loneliness and isolation among youth

f. the draft and the war

g. poverty, especially in minority groups like Negroes and migrant workers

Is the Church doing anything about these? Should it, for example, organize education programs in narcotics, start programs to bring youth and their parents closer together, promote crime enforcement, picket movie houses showing smutty movies, sponsor dances for kids, organize draft resistance movements, start welfare agencies?

If it does, it certainly should not become some highly organized political and economic force.

What it should do is take a clear stand on these issues, basing its reasons on the Gospels, and then teach these positions to the members of the Church. From then on it is up to individuals to organize as they see fit—not as Catholics, but as concerned human beings, to do whatever must be done to aid man and bring him into friendship with others.

Has the Church Failed?

If it has failed, it has failed in terms of not taking clear stands and sufficiently encouraging its members to get out into society and live the Gospel.

On the other hand, often the Church has done just this, but the individual members never got off their pants to put the Gospel ideas into action on their own.

So before we complain that the Church isn't doing anything, we have to be sure that we are willing to do something, for it is really the people within the Church who are supposed to change society, by their individual and cooperative efforts within society.

Summary

The Church has a mission—to help men realize the dream of the Gospel.

It goes about fulfilling this mission primarily by simply teaching and giving example of what the Gospel says.

It was never intended to be a "social service agency." The Church is people who share a dream. It is up to us as individuals to make that dream a reality within our own sphere of influence. We aren't supposed to wait until the Church sponsors some "Catholic project" to act.

So if the Church is not reaching youth, the real problem lies with the youth who are already within the Church, people like yourselves. Actually no one has more influence—either good or bad—on youth than their high school classmates. If some youth don't share the dream of the Gospel, it is rather hopeless to expect that others will pick it up and live it.

So to talk about the mission of the Church to youth, for example, is to talk about your mission. That is, if you regard yourself as a member of the Church.

Note that we aren't talking about pious organizations—just kids being with kids. But if some of the kids have a dream it is bound to rub off on others.

THE CHURCH'S MISSION

TH GRADE GROUPS

1   What are some of the biggest problems ninth grade students face? Does the dream for man contained in the Gospel offer a solution to these problems?

2   Do ninth grade students have a role in the mission of the Church? How would you "announce" the Gospel to your classmates? What would happen if you tried it? Do you think you would need help from a group like this?

3   What part of the Gospel speaks loudest to high school students? Why? What part turns off most high school students?

4   Do you think the Church has done a good job of teaching the Gospel to high school students? How has it failed? How has it succeeded? What should it do now?

5   If the Church shouldn't be involved in politics and in things like that, how do you think it should attempt to share its dream for man with the world?

6   If the real work of the Church is to keep alive the dream that Jesus had for all men, is it keeping this dream alive? Is any other group doing the same thing or doing it better?

7   Is it realistic to expect individuals to carry out the job of correcting social problems instead of relying on the organization of the Church to do this? For example, should individuals organize a peace movement or should the Church do this and demand that its members participate?

8   Can you really expect ninth grade students to get excited about social injustice, war in Vietnam, or the race problem? What kinds of things should we expect ninth grade students to get excited about and work for?

9   If you either individually or as a group do not influence your classmates and help shape the future of your school, who will? Can you afford to just sit back and let others shape your future for you?

10   Can the Church really help high school students? Can high school students really help the Church? Do you think this group is a part of the Church? Does this group have any responsibility to announce the Gospel to the high school world? How should it go about it?

THE CHURCH'S MISSION

10
TH GRADE GROUPS

1   If the Church's only role in the world is to keep alive the Gospel dream among men, has it succeeded? To what degree? Insofar as it has failed to some degree, why do you think it fails? Why does it fail among high school students? What is the best way to teach the Gospel to high school students?

2   If you agree that youth have the most influence over youth, then it would follow that the best ones to teach the Gospel to youth are other young people? Is this realistic? How could you teach the Gospel to your classmates? How could this group teach the Gospel to others?

3   If the Church is not supposed to be involved in politics or in practical movements like the peace movement, in any organized way, what kind of responsibility does that place on individual Catholics like yourselves?

4   What are some of the key problems high school students face today? Does the Gospel speak to them about these problems and give them any hope or solutions? Should the Church become more involved with the problems of youth or is it the task of youth to work out these solutions with the help of the Church?

5   Is there any cause or movement today that really speaks to you, one that you would like to become involved in (like the peace movement, the racial, or poverty question)? Do you think in doing so you would be announcing the Gospel? What would you be announcing?

6   Would you consider our group here part of the Church? If we are, what is our responsibility in regard to announcing the Gospel? Why doesn't the idea turn high school students on? Are we too young to get concerned yet about big issues in society? Should high school students just go to school, participate in school activities and wait until they are in the adult world before they get involved?

7   How would you rate our town—as a great place to live or as a dead place? How alive do you think the Gospel dream is in our town? Is the Church here doing anything significant to shape the city according to the dream of the Gospel? Can you individually or as a group do anything *now* to shape our town? Should you, as high school students, even be concerned?

8   Youth is always inspired by a cause and a challenge. Does the Gospel dream give you such a cause? If not, why not?

9   Can you think of any really great Christians today? What are they doing? Are there many in our town? Are they among the high school group?

10 At what age do you think people become responsible for the shape society is in? Is it fair for high school students to complain about the mess they "inherited" from their parents? Is this an excuse for noninvolvement?

THE CHURCH'S MISSION

11

TH GRADE GROUPS

1 If the Church's only role in the world is to keep alive the Gospel dream among men, has it succeeded? To what degree? Insofar as it has failed to some degree, why do you think it fails? Why does it fail among high school students? What is the best way to teach the Gospel to high school students?

2 If you agree that youth have the most influence over youth, then it would follow that the best ones to teach the Gospel to youth are other young people. Is this realistic? How could you teach the Gospel to your classmates? How could this group teach the Gospel to others?

3 If the Church is not supposed to be involved in politics or in practical movements like the peace movement, in any organized way, what kind of responsibility does that place on individual Catholics like yourselves?

4   What are some of the key problems high school students face today? Does the Gospel speak to them about these problems and give them any hope or solutions? Should the Church become more involved with the problems of youth or is it the task of youth to work out these solutions with the help of the Church?

5   Is there any cause or movement today that really speaks to you, one that you would like to become involved in? (Like the peace movement, the racial question, etc.?) Do you think in doing so you would be announcing the Gospel? What would you be announcing?

6   Would you consider our group here part of the Church? If we are, what is our responsibility in regard to announcing the Gospel? Why does the idea so often turn high school students off? Are we too young to get concerned yet about big issues in society? Should high school students just go to school, participate in school activities and wait until they are in the adult world before they get involved?

7   How would you rate our town—as a great place to live or as a dead place? How alive do you think the Gospel is here? Is the Church here doing anything significant to shape the people according to the dream of the Gospel? Can you individually or as a group do anything *now* to shape our town? Should you, as high school students, even be concerned?

8   Youth is always inspired by a cause and a challenge. Does the Gospel dream give you such a cause? If not, why not?

9   Can you think of any really great Christians today? What are they doing? Are there many in our town? Are they among the high school group?

10   At what age do you think people become responsible for the shape society is in? Is it fair for high school students to complain about the mess they "inherited" from their parents?

CELEBRATING LIFE

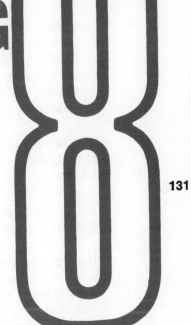

The goal of the session is for the students to see the relationship between the celebrations they are used to and Church celebrations or sacraments. Also to give the students a better understanding of the nature and purpose of celebrations in human life.

I. BEGINNING EXERCISE

The purpose of this exercise is to have the students become more aware of the elements of a celebration and the nature of celebration, as a preparation for discussing the sacraments as forms of celebration—with emphasis on the Mass.

Instructions:

1. Give each person a kit containing a penny balloon, a piece of string, a few jelly beans, or similar inexpensive candy, and several sheets of plain white paper, like typing

paper. Use an old brown bag or something to contain the
kit. Have on hand some crayons or colored marking
pencils, and something like scotch tape or a stapler. (You
can enlarge the kit at your discretion.)

2. After they have examined the contents of their kit,
instruct them that we want to plan a celebration. We are
celebrating the fact that this is the last class. They must
decide how to use all the items they have been given as
part of the celebrations, and they must decide just what
they are going to do by way of celebrating.

For example, they may want to use the balloons to
decorate the room, the paper and string to make masks,
the candy to use as gifts to each other, etc.

Or they may want to use the balloons for a contest, the
paper to make hats, the candy to use for the refreshments.

However, they have one special goal. Whatever they
decide to do must in some way *express or symbolize* how
they feel about what they are celebrating—the end of
class; thus, they must try to symbolize for example, the
friendships they have formed, what they feel they have
learned, the fact they will soon be "free" again, etc.

3. After they have discussed for a while just what they would
do to celebrate, using the available materials, they should
then act it out briefly.

4. Afterwards, you should begin the discussion and
instruction about what the celebration is, how they feel
about celebrations, and then go into the nature of the
Church celebrations to see the comparisons, differences,
weaknesses, etc. (See the instruction and questions on
celebration.)

II. STUDENT REACTION

III. INSTRUCTION AND DISCUSSION

(The outline for the formal instruction and discussion questions can be found at the end of this lesson.)

BREAK PERIOD

IV. SECOND EXERCISE

There is no second exercise planned. Instead you may want to actually plan a class party, or you may want to discuss plans for having a class liturgy. Or you may simply want to extend the break and have a party.

Before the group breaks up, ask them to fill out the evaluation forms which will be provided before your last meeting.

INSTRUCTION ON CELEBRATING LIFE

(Note to adult leader: *The outline below is intended as a sample outline. To be effective, it must be developed and adapted by you, that is, put into your own words and style and filled out with sufficient examples from your own and the students' experience.*)

Introduction

134 In our activity and discussion we tried to get an insight into what makes up a celebration. Since celebration is a very important part of human life, it usually becomes an integral part of the life of any group.

For example, our country celebrates certain days like the Fourth of July, since it symbolizes an important value for our country, our independence.

Every group tends to develop its own celebrations for its own reasons. The Church, as a group of people, is no different. As our final effort to explore the Church, we want to see how the Church as a group celebrates.

What the Church Celebrates

Usually a group celebrates the most significant things that happen to it. That's why families celebrate birthdays, wedding anniversaries, graduations, etc.

The most significant thing that happened to the Church is Jesus. So the Church celebrates Jesus, or more specifically, what Jesus has done for the Church.

The main thing Jesus did is promise us eternal life, and he did this himself by conquering death. So the Church celebrates the fact that Jesus has conquered death and that he still lives with us.

That is really what the Mass is all about. By signs like bread and wine and the words of the Last Supper, the Church recalls that

Jesus died for us and rose again and is now present under these signs to help us learn how to live.

The Church celebrates other things too, like the fact that God forgives us. The Sacrament of Reconciliation (Penance) is really a celebration of God's forgiveness of us.

Each sacrament in turn is a particular celebration of what Jesus does for us: Baptism celebrates our entrance into the Church, for example.

How the Church Celebrates

The Church has a few set rules for celebrating much like we have certain rules for a birthday party, like cake and candles:

1. Some key person, in most instances a priest trained and ordained for the purpose, serves as master of ceremonies —much like the father usually presides over a family celebration.

2. Certain key words and actions are usually a part of the celebration and are intended to help us realize what and why we are celebrating. For example, the words of consecration at Mass recall the Last Supper.

3. Certain key materials are used as part of the celebration, the most obvious being bread and wine at Mass, since the Mass symbolizes a banquet-type celebration or meal.

4. Since these are always intended to be a community celebration, you always need people. Without people it would be like having your own birthday party alone in your room.

Unfortunately, celebrations like the Mass have lost much of their celebration mood over the centuries. They are often dull, monotonous, and unreal. They really don't seem to capture the spirit of what we are celebrating: the fact that Jesus is with us and we will live forever.

There are a lot of reasons for this and we won't go into them now, the fact is that most Church celebrations, especially the Mass, seldom come through as real, human, joyful celebrations full of fun and also significance. Most of us seem to go out of habit or out of a sense of obligation. Seldom do people seem to come to Mass with the idea of celebrating something.

Why the Church Celebrates

The Church, like any group, celebrates for several reasons:

1. Simply because they have something to celebrate, some joy or some event that they want to "shout about."

2. Also we celebrate to try to recapture what has already happened and in a sense make it happen again. That's why Christians have always been convinced that at Mass Jesus truly comes in a special way into our midst, just as he was with the apostles, and in coming he shares his new life with us.

3. A celebration is also a good way for people to learn. For example, when the U.S. celebrates the Fourth of July with parades and speeches, we all get a chance to recall and to learn more about how good it is to live in a free country. So celebrations can also teach us something.

   The readings and homily at Mass are intended to do that, but it is obvious they don't always work.

Summary and Application

The Church, like any human community, has some regular celebrations.

We call them sacraments and liturgy.

The main thing the Church celebrates is Jesus and what he has done for us: given us eternal life.

For all kinds of reasons, Church celebrations today don't seem much like celebrations, and they aren't too popular, especially with people your age.

Nonetheless, the potential is still there. Jesus still makes himself present at these celebrations: We still have something to celebrate; we still have the need and the urge to celebrate.

The real question seems to be: How can we make these Church celebrations what they once were and what they are intended to be—real, joyful, human celebrations in which we recall what Jesus has done, learn more about what Jesus has done, and make it happen all over in our midst?

CELEBRATING LIFE

QUESTIONS

138

9 10 11
GRADE GROUPS

1   What kinds of things do most students like to
celebrate? What are some common elements in every
celebration? Does every man really need to celebrate
occasionally at least?

2   What do you think is the main reason Church
celebrations don't seem to come off as celebrations? Do
people know what they are celebrating? Do you think
most people at Mass even know that they are celebrating?
Is it a problem of too many people, not enough time,
outdated language and symbols, too many celebrations?
What?

3   Do you think people your age could ever have fun at a
Church celebration? What would it take to make the
Mass a joyful, fun-filled experience and at the same time
keep it as worship of God? Do you think many young
people know, care or understand that the Church is
celebrating the fact that we will live forever?

4   Have you ever had fun at Mass, felt it was a real celebration? Can you tell us what took place that made you feel that way?

5   What do you think, besides music, ninth grade students have to offer at Mass that could help make it a real celebration and not just a dead ritual? (Tenth and eleventh grade students?)

6   Lots of high school students have stopped going to Mass, at least regularly. Why? Do you blame them? What would it take to get them to come again?

7   What is the best celebration you ever experienced? How old were you? Who was involved? What did you do?

8   Do you think this group should try to put on a Church celebration—that is, ask a priest to come and celebrate a Mass with us? What would you want to do at this Mass? Who would you want to take part? Do you think we really could celebrate the fact that we will live forever? Are we really convinced enough of that—that we want to celebrate it? What other things do we have that we could celebrate together? Can we really mix religion and fun?

9   True celebrations are always done with at least one other person and the best ones involve a group of people. Do you agree? Do you need others to help you celebrate? Can you celebrate alone? Why do you think we usually need others to help us celebrate?

10 What would happen to a community like the Church if it stopped having common celebrations of the key events that happened to it, like Easter, Christmas, Pentecost, etc.? Can we really celebrate these events if we don't understand how they have and are affecting us today? Do most Christians really believe enough in the fact that we will live forever?

ADDITIONAL
READINGS
AND
SUGGESTIONS

The following selections are samples of the kind of material that is available today almost everywhere. You will probably be able to add many other selections of your own to these readings.

They can be used in several ways in the sessions in this handbook. First, you may wish to incorporate quotes chosen from the readings to make a point in your formal presentation of the lesson. Or you may wish to read the selection first and then give your formal presentation by way of explaining the reading. Or you may wish to close the evening with the reading, presenting it as a kind of summary of what was discussed throughout the evening, a kind of "thought to take home with you."

Since the readings are selected at random, they will not be appropriate for all age groups. Some will be too deep for freshmen, others may be too shallow for juniors. Use your own judgment in this matter.

Another source of supplementary readings, of course, is Scripture. You should have little difficulty selecting a parable or passage from an Epistle which could be used as a summary of the evening.

Some tips about using readings:

1. They should never last more than a minute or two.

2. Always prepare the reading ahead of time and edit it to suit your purpose—for example, changing the word "love" to "respect" if that will go over better in the group.

3. Don't ask a student to read for you unless you have "practiced" with him beforehand to insure that it is read well and with an element of comprehension and sincerity.

4. Don't *depend* upon the reading to stimulate discussion; it should be *part of several* things you do to provide content and stimulate discussion.

5. After finishing a reading, ask the students if they would like to hear part or all of it again so they are sure they understood it.

6. To capture attention at the beginning, say something significant about the reading and if possible raise an initial question. Examples would be:

   a. "Here is what a student your age wrote about what we are discussing. See if you agree with him."

   b. "Maybe this reading will summarize all we've been saying all night. See if it says what you would like to say."

OTHER
SUPPLEMENTARY
AIDS

With a little imagination—or by asking one or two of your
students to help you ahead of time—you can often come up with
a popular record that says something about the topic. For
example, *Impossible Dream* from the musical play *Man From
La Mancha,* or the recording of Martin Luther King's speech
"I Have a Dream" would fit well into your session on dreaming.

Also, magazines are filled with pictures which will often capture
the main theme of the evening. By asking a few students to make
some posters ahead of time, you can create an atmosphere by
placing these around the room and call attention to them at an
appropriate time.

RESPECT

MAN TOGETHER: FOUNDATION OF BROTHERHOOD

One of the most beautiful words in the English language is "we." What *I* cannot accomplish, *we* can do with ease. Alone, man is locked in the frustration of forces he is unable to control. Man together is man liberated from the prison of self. Man with others is man encouraged, man with hope, man alive!

The world cries out in anguish to have unity among men. Every demonstration for civil rights is a plea for the brotherhood of man. Every sign of "flower power" is a cry for the power of love that can unite the hearts of men and make them one.

Yet, man who strains to be one, often breaks the bonds that make him one with other men. Where is the sign that tells man that brotherhood is more than a desperate and futile dream?

The seed of brotherhood is planted in the heart of every man. It buds forth in the relationships that exist among men. Every interpersonal relationship points to what can be in the community of man. A man who cannot speak even to one man cannot speak with all men. Each person we meet is a reflection of the community of man. Our ability to relate with the individual gives us hope.

Love and understanding are not impossible dreams. We are surrounded by persons who love one another: the mother who loves her child, the sweethearts that make a pact of their love in marriage. All these are signs of what we can be when we are together. Love is not easy. Love is demanding. Love asks what seems impossible and makes it possible.

The mystery of brotherhood is contained in love itself. Only the man who has loved one can love many. Never to have loved one is never to have loved. The experience of love generates new relationships. The greater the love, the larger the embrace. Man who loves much hugs the world in the embrace of true fellowship. Observe young lovers. They are incapable of hate. They are enamored of the world and the world's possibilities. They have a dream. They have a vision. The world needs dreamers, visionaries who can live with the hope of the future and make it present.

Man meets man in many ways. He relates to other men on the superficial level, for instance. A walk through a supermarket is an enlightening experience. The way a person treats the girl at the checkout counter says many things. How a woman reacts to being overcharged is significant. If she can place the incident into an objective prospective and still respect the girl who has overcharged her, she is well on her way.

How we relate to our neighbors is important. The respect with which we treat one another is a sign of our regard for them. The mailman is more than an object that delivers mail. The waitress is more than an object that serves food. Recognizing others as persons who have needs like ours, persons who need to be loved and listened to, paves the way for more interpersonal relationships. Obviously, we cannot relate interpersonally with hundreds of persons. Sheer numbers defeat us. We must, though, recognize in each person the potential of an interpersonal relationship. This recognition enables us to treat others as persons with worth and to recognize the relationships that they have with other persons. Magnified by the millions of people in the world the possibilities are exciting.

Each Eucharist is a sign of what man can be. Held together by the love of the Father, man is able to see in other men the exciting dynamic of brotherhood. Fellowship depends on each of us. What is happening in the world is merely a reflection of what is happening on the level of the person. No wonder that countries cannot get along when people are not relating. Everything in man cries out for unity. This shout is reflected in the peace movement, the civil rights movement, and other movements that speak for the dignity of man.

Each of us must work for fellowship with those with whom we live. Lucy's argument that she loves mankind and hates people doesn't hold for us. It is virtually impossible to work for the good of mankind without working for the good of people.—(Rev. Theodore Stone)

CORE MORALITY

I figure my ideal is someone who is really happy in what he is doing. When I say "really" I mean to say intrinsically, deep down, because that's where it counts.

Now this guy who is happy can be anything. A truck driver, a politician, a teacher—anything. And he's happy because he's doing what he has to do because he wants to do it, and not merely because he has to do it.

I suppose this guy must be living up to his potential and all that, but that's really part of it. I doubt seriously that a man could be happy knowing he could be doing something on another plane which he could do better. Someone like that more than likely would be discontented—a characteristic which does not breed happiness.

And this word "happiness" is not exactly right either. It sort of connotes walking around with a stupid grin on your face all day. There are pain and sorrow in life, but when a man is fulfilled in what he is doing, the pain and the sorrow take on a perspective essentially the same as joy and good times.

You see there's a core inside all of us, and if it's rotted because of discontent, because of fear to know ourselves, the taste of our lives is bad when we are alone and thinking. But if the core is full and rich, the taste of our lives is sweet in moments of solitude. When all shame is stripped, my ideal knows that it was worth it to be born, because he is filled up inside with the acceptance of himself and the dignity of his person.—(A High School Senior, *Discovery in Word,* Robert Heyer, S.J., et al., p. 116, Paulist Press, 1968)

Some Questions:

"And he's happy because he's doing what he has to do because he wants to do it . . ." Is there anyone you know who has been able to do this? Is he happy?

". . . the pain and the sorrow take on a perspective essentially the same as joy and good times." What does this mean? Do you believe fulfillment can do this?

How do you feel about your life when you are alone, and thinking? Do you think about it much? Was it worth it to be born?

HAPPINESS AND TEILHARD DE CHARDIN

The individual, if he is to fulfill and preserve himself, must strive to break down every barrier that prevents separate beings from uniting. His is the exaltation, not of egotistical autonomy but of communion with all others! Essentially the Universe is narrowing to a centre, like the successive layers of a cone: It is convergent in structure.—(*The Future of Man,* Teilhard de Chardin, p. 46, Harper & Row)

Some Questions:

Why is communion with others so important for the happiness
of all men?

In what way are happiness and hope shown to be part of the
same expression in Teilhard's words?

PERSONAL FULFILLMENT

I just can't make ideals and realities part of the same story.
I mean I have an idea of how I should act with a girl, but the
whole thing gets all fouled up when the two of you are sitting
there making out. Or when you know damn well you're
supposed to give—for to give is to love—and when the times
come you hold your breath till the situation is past, and then gasp
and say, "Too bad about that." And I see the ideals of the people
who have lived longer than I have, and I hear their sweet words
and their mellow aphorisms but know too well their less-than-
virtuous actions to believe. And so I am suspicious. Of them. Of
myself. Of others. And it becomes hard to believe sometimes. To
believe even what you think is the truth, what you feel inside is
the real thing. Now I'm not saying I don't believe anything.
That's ridiculous. But it becomes harder to say the ideal is right
when too, too many believe that the reality, practical and
material and possibly shallow, is right.

I think to be a Christian man, a guy has to decide if he's going to
play it the way he knows it should be played, or play it the way
the guy next to him is playing it—and making out just fine. I
figure that's where Jesus comes in, with the strength to make the
right decision, and someone to look at who made it by playing it
straight.—(A High School Senior, *Discovery in Word,* Robert
Heyer, S.J., et al., p. 119, Paulist Press, 1968)

SUPPLEMENTARY
READING

FREEDOM

"THE WAY IT IS"

"I don't talk to them much." The idea is to talk with your parents, to make your point as clearly as you can and then listen to theirs. Don't get bitchy and play put-ons. That achieves nothing. If they just don't understand, and you're tired of hearing "Well, you have to admit, son, that your mother and I have lived a lot longer than you have," then try to play it so you can get on without hurting them, until the time comes when things have mellowed, or you are old enough to make it on your own. But the truth is what is, and they have, as a matter of fact, lived a lot longer than you have. This doesn't mean they understand you, but it probably does mean that they understand the world you've got to live in, and which the average American youth has only a vague notion of. You can know things are lousy and corrupt, but that's not to say you know how to go about paying bills on a new house and raising a family that needs a lot of love and looking after. In some cases at least, and only the person can judge them, lack of experience should yield the benefit of the doubt.

"I do not like being stamped as one of a large group when nobody bothers to find out whether I am a person."

Are you? A person I mean. Because the last time I asked you, out came the defense and up went the hands. "Hey, look—just don't try to pin me down." And you went over to sulk in the corner and play chords on your guitar (or flip baseball cards with yourself or whatever you do over in a corner sulking).
"You don't know how it is, man."
"Okay, then how is it?"   **151**
"I don't know. I mean I can't explain it. You know."
"Yeah. I know."
And here's the way it is:

Now y'see before I met this girl when I was 15, the only person I ever really talked to was a kid in school. We were sitting down on the steps and he asked me if he could ask me something, and I said, "Sure." He wanted to know if girls masturbate. I didn't know, but we started talking, and I told him all sorts of things about what I felt. We talked for a long time. And when I saw him the next day, it was no good. Like we knew too much about each other. We didn't talk like that anymore. It was no good.

Nobody really cares, you find that out. Your time comes for your 15 minutes in the student counselor's office, and he talks about what you ought to do in life, like you're not even there and he's talking to the whole student body heart to heart. And he doesn't know you want to talk about being lonely, or how sometimes you can't cry and you want to, really bad. But he wouldn't understand.

And how many times were you with somebody who really gave a damn about what you had to say, about your girl and about the game? Twice?

Look. Nobody cares. You find that out. You find that out pretty damn quick in this world.

O.K. But if you want people to care, you have to start by caring about them. Listen to them, find what's good in them, understand their faults. If you brood, if you turn cynical, if you really couldn't give a damn about anybody else, you're a drag. And nobody will care very much whether or not you want to be stamped as part of one large group. It's just taken for granted.— (*Discovery in Word,* Robert Heyer, S.J., et al., pp. 25-28, Paulist Press, 1968)

NECESSITY FOR DREAMING

MAN'S SEARCH FOR MEANING

We who lived in concentration camps can remember the men who walked through the huts comforting others, giving away their last piece of bread. They may have been few in number, but they offer sufficient proof that everything can be taken from a man but one thing: the last of the human freedoms—to choose one's attitude in any given set of circumstances, to choose one's own way.

And there were always choices to make. Every day, every hour, offered the opportunity to make a decision, a decision which determined whether you would or would not submit to those powers which threatened to rob you of your very self, your inner freedom; which determined whether or not you would become the plaything of circumstance, renouncing freedom and dignity to become molded into the form of the typical inmate.

Seen from this point of view, the mental reactions of the inmates of a concentration camp must seem more to us than the mere expression of certain physical and sociological conditions. Even though conditions such as lack of sleep, insufficient food and various mental stresses may suggest that the inmates were bound to react in certain ways, in the final analysis it becomes clear that the sort of person the prisoner became was the result of an inner decision, and not the result of camp influences alone. Fundamentally, therefore, any man can, even under such circumstances, decide what shall become of him—mentally and spiritually. He may retain his human dignity even in a concentration camp. Dostoevski said once, "There is only one thing that I dread: not to be worthy of my sufferings." These words frequently came to my mind after I became acquainted with those martyrs whose behavior in camp, whose suffering and death, bore witness to the fact that the last inner freedom cannot be lost. It can be said that they were worthy of their sufferings; the way they bore their suffering was a genuine inner achievement. It is this spiritual freedom—which cannot be taken away—that makes life meaningful and purposeful.—(*Man's Search for Meaning,* Viktor Frankl, pp. 64-65, Beacon Press, 1959, 1962)

154

THE GOSPEL DREAM

THE IMPOSSIBLE DREAM

I know, I know, man will answer. I have tested the scriptures too. But when I want to say, "I believe," I can only say, "I want to believe." Want to—do you hear? I want to believe like a shepherd or a king—or a sinner. But where in the world is He? No one is there. The whole world is like an empty stage set, an empty creche. The center, the poet says, falls apart. No one stands there. No one is born. So the kings pack up their gifts and go off wearily, the shepherds melt back into the crowd, the children grow distracted and run off. The faithful go elsewhere— some in faith, some in regret.

I hope we never lose hope. That would be the tragedy. That would be the drought; all the wells and watersheds of the world down to dry rock. Every man his own policeman and his neighbor's enemy, every man building his bomb and guarding his bomb shelter, armed to the teeth. Such a world, I hope, Christ would indeed flee. . . .

I hope all bombs dissolve into butter for hungry men.

I hope (imagine!) this year—no one dies! No one dies. I mean, in the final glacial death—into hopelessness, into violence, into power that is empty of conscience, into dread and nausea and inaction and egoism and base fear.

> Sing it out—all the graveyards gone!
> Sing it out—enough light to go by!
> Sing it out—enough brothers to live for!
> Sing it out, Jesus Son of Man—we can make it!—

(D. Berrigan, S.J., "Where in the World Is He?" *Jesuit Missions,* March, 1966)

Some Questions:

What is the message of hope expressed here by Daniel Berrigan? What hope do you envision for the happiness of man?

The longer I live, the more I feel that true repose consists in "renouncing" one's own self, by which I mean making up one's mind to admit that there is no importance whatever in being "happy" or "unhappy" in the usual meaning of the words. Personal success and personal satisfaction are not worth another thought if one does achieve them, or worth worrying about if they evade one or are slow in coming. All that is really worthwhile is action—faithful action, for the world, and in God.

Before one can see that and live by it, there is a sort of threshold to cross, or a reversal to be made in what appears to be man's general habit of thought; but once that gesture has been made, what freedom is yours, freedom to work and to love!—(*Letters From a Traveller,* Teilhard de Chardin, p. 160, Harper & Row)

Question:

How, practically, does one "renounce" himself? "All that is really worthwhile is action." Why?

In place of a reading you might want to play the song, "The Impossible Dream" from the musical, *Man from La Mancha*. The words are very meaningful in relation to this lesson.

THE CHURCH

MAN BECOMES

The wonder of life is the possibility of what mankind can become. All life is a "becoming." The seed becomes a flower. The acorn becomes an oak. The boy becomes a man. The student becomes a professor. All this in an exciting and dynamic movement toward! That this is rooted in the heart of man is obvious from even the small child who is always talking about what he is "going to be." "What is" is frequently not as exciting as "What will be."

Man does not move forward alone. The single step of the infant is the result of the coaching and coaxing of infinitely patient and loving parents. What man can become is, in many ways, conditioned by what other people think he can be. The wonder of what happens when man is trusted and encouraged is marvelous to behold. He becomes, in a sense, what another has believed that he could be. This is the power of a friend, someone who knows you through and through, and believes in you still.

The community of man is like this, too. The potential of man together can be activated only by a community that believes in itself. Large groups of scientists all over the world are researching the possibilities of a cure for cancer because the world believes that it can be done. Man will reach the moon because the world is sure that man can do it.

All life demands change. Unless the seed dies, new life cannot become. Man must be open to change or there can be no growth. Not to advance is to step backwards. Man has to be willing to be insecure so that a greater security can come about.

Modern society is in constant flux. New scientific and technological discoveries have changed the tempo of our life. The persons we love are no further away than our telephones. What is happening on the other side of the world enters our living rooms every evening on the news broadcasts.

Man's life span is increasing. What was once old age is now middle age. The useful years of a man's life have increased. Each change demands other changes. Because man lives longer, the potential of old age must be explored.

The Church exists within the world. The changes of the world become changes for the Church. Each new understanding of man as a person demands a response within the Church. The liturgy of yesterday is not the liturgy of today. The growth in understanding of the human community promotes understanding of the Christian community.

If the thoughts of men and women become freer, and they begin to cast off old hang-ups and ignore moral taboos that have proved themselves the essence of immorality, then the organization which serves those men and women must also change, or be left as a quaint piece of memorabilia. The Christian

Church has not only opted to throw aside the childish and the antiquated, but to take the forefront in moral growth, and act as an influence and an impetus for change among all men.—(Rev. Theodore Stone)

The "cult of stuffiness" in the Church is under fire from Msgr. George W. Casey, syndicated columnist, who would like to see us "give up a good deal of our stuffiness." He explains: "By this is meant that whole amazing establishment of vesture, headdress, staffs, thrones, canopies, coats of arms, titles, genuflections, ring-kissing, deferences, processional order, protocol, etc., that characterizes official people in our Church and distinguishes them from anything else in the world save, perhaps, the British court at a time of coronation or maybe some small oriental court left over somewhere from the Middle Ages. It gets more space in the code of canon law than the rights of man, and it means more to some people than the gospel."—(D. Herr, *Overview*, July 15, 1967)

Some Questions:

What is meant by the "cult of stuffiness"? How has stuffiness impaired the freedom not only of clerics but of parishioners as well?

Do you think that all ritual should be done away with?

Have some Christian symbols lost their meaning? What are some of the symbols in the Church that should be kept, and which still connote something rich to the Christian?

Is natural symbolism, such as water for cleansing and white for purity, still valid today?

If change is part of life, change is part of the Church. The question: "When will the changes in the Church end?" can only be answered, "When the changes in man end." Obviously, this is not going to happen. Change is part of growth. One proof of the living, growing dynamism of the Church is change.

To change is to suffer. The Church, because it is a growing dynamism, has growing pains. Not all the members of the Church are willing to suffer. Some are unwilling to die so that they might rise. As the seed dies, so the flower can become; man must die so that he can have life most abundantly.

To change is to grow. To change is to put away the security of childhood. The Church must not become man's "security blanket" or growth will be stifled. There is a security in change, the security that we are becoming. This is all the adult Christian needs. To know that we are moving forward is enough.

How can we be sure that change is growth? In the Church, we have the promise of the Father, who sent his Son so that death could be the promise of new life—so that suffering could have meaning. Suffering is the by-product of change and growth. Christ suffered to give meaning to man's living. Faith gives meaning to life. Our belief in what is helps us to believe in what will be. All man is caught in a movement toward the parousia—the fullness of life in eternity.

FREEDOM AND CHURCH

I go to church because my parents want me to. If they didn't make me, I probably would still go, but I can't be sure. I don't listen when I go now. I spend the time daydreaming. I don't know if I'm insulting God but I don't think so, because I know my greatest belief is in God. What I want out of religion is to figure out a code by which I should live. I have none right now, and I can't just accept somebody else's. When I was little, everything came naturally. Now everything seems so complex. However, being 100-per-cent secure is dead. When you are insecure, at least you are alive. I hope people will never become so narrow that they will start worshiping the thing that is created rather than the Creator. A lot of people do that right now by worshiping money. I don't want a lot of money. If you have a million dollars when you die, it doesn't make you a better person. —(A student, "The Separate World of Youth," *The Young Americans,* p. 44, Time-Life Books, 1966)

Some Questions:

What are your reasons for going to church?

". . . my greatest belief is in God." What is your greatest belief in? Do you really believe in anything?

How are faith and freedom related?

THE CHURCH'S MISSION

YOUTH LOOKING AT YOUTH

So many (teenagers) could really do something for the world, but they're just sitting around doing nothing. Magazines and newspapers seem to take two types of teenagers, high-society types and hoodlums, and say "this is the American teenager." They don't seem to think the middle and lower classes have anything to offer. But this is the largest category, in between, the kids who don't have hot rods to run around in, but don't have to steal to eat. What I'm afraid of is that the teenagers of today, when they grow older, will be just like the adults of today. They don't let brotherly love come through. If that's the future, then the world's in pretty bad shape.—(*The Young Americans,* p. 12, Time-Life Books, 1966)

Some Questions:

"What I'm afraid of is that the teenagers of today, when they grow older, will be just like the adults of today." What is the one thing that will assure his fear being realized?

How good is the communication among teenagers themselves? Do they understand each other, or is that a game too, mouthing lines from both Dylans and paying empty verbal homage to Kahlil Gibran and Jesus Christ, and filling in the lull in the conversation with, "Isn't *The Lord of the Rings* tremendous?"

When you talk deep (as it is so called) are you really trying to transfer an idea, an emotion, to another person, or are you just doing a good imitation of what you think someone deep should say?

What does he mean when he says, "They don't let brotherly love come through"?

CELEBRATING LIFE

MAN RESPONDS IN WONDER

Life is a *reason* for celebration! Life *is* a celebration! The wonder of every new beat of man's heart reflected in a pulse gives joy that asks for celebration. The joy of discovering a daisy, or even a dandelion, sends hope surging into the heart of a man who is aware.

Delight and awareness are in the heart of every child. The three-year-old whose question is always "Why?" and the eleven-year-old who is caught in delight at the sight of a butterfly speak to man the message of life. To the adult observer the message is: Come alive! Be alive! Respond to life!

Within the heart of a child is the embryo of what an adult is capable of being and seldom is. The child responds to life. The adult, too often, is so caught up in struggling for existence and in the pedestrian concerns of everyday life that he misses the pulse of "what can be" in his concern for what actually is. Excitement is a possibility. The chrysalis is exciting because of the butterfly that will be. The acorn vibrates with the life of the oak. What is more exciting than the feel of an unborn baby kicking? Nothing is more exciting than what can be!

Each of us must develop the awareness of the child. We must look with eyes that see and hear with ears attuned to the joy of life. Man who is must come alive with the possibility of man who can be.

What gives man wonder? The possibilities are endless. Man can be moved to respond to the glories of nature: a sunrise, sunset, an insect, a tree, a flower, a path through the woods. He can be moved by art, architecture, literature, films; but, most of all, he is moved by people.

Each of man's responses is a "yes" to life. Man's response is within him. It struggles to be voiced. It wiggles within until it is set free in a word, in a song, in a gesture. The wonder of man's response is like a telegraph message sending vibrations to the whole of humanity. It bubbles forth in a giggle, leaps out in a shout, responds in the thunder of an alleluia. Man is meant to explode in song, burst forth with poetry, and kneel in prayer.

When man responds with other men, the celebration becomes more complex, more moving, and even more meaningful. The contagion of laughter or tears makes for community response. No one has to tell the community when to weep or when to laugh. Those celebrations are necessary. The sorrow of an entire world was caught up in a single collective tear at the time of the deaths of Martin Luther King and Robert Kennedy. The tear cried for expression and the world liturgized in front of countless television screens and in thousands of churches and synagogues. How does man respond with other men? Spontaneity cries for form and structure. Liturgy results. The liturgy of life is life, life made reasonable by understanding and response.

The Christian, too, responds. He responds to the happiness of having been given an awareness of the beauty of life and an inkling of what is to come. Like all men, he responds within and his response is caught in the collective response of all Christians. The Christian's response is the expression of what is possible in the life of every man. His Eucharist is a thanksgiving for what is and an alleluia of what will be. His celebration uses the very "stuff of life" and makes it holy. It is because the Christian has participated in the many small celebrations of life that he can participate in this largest of all celebrations, the Eucharist. It is the poem, the song, the shout, the moan, and the tear that give man an understanding of the Eucharist and give him something about which to be Eucharistic. Christ becomes our celebration. He becomes our Eucharist. He becomes both the reason for celebration and celebration itself.—(Rev. Theodore Stone)